# MUTUAL FUND INVESTING

*Comprehensive Beginner's Guide to Learn the Basics and Effective Methods of Mutual Fund Investing*

CHARLIE EVANS

© Copyright 2019 - All rights reserved.

The content contained within this book may not be reproduced, duplicated or transmitted without direct written permission from the author or the publisher.

Under no circumstances will any blame or legal responsibility be held against the publisher, or author, for any damages, reparation, or monetary loss due to the information contained within this book. Either directly or indirectly.

Legal Notice:

This book is copyright protected. This book is only for personal use. You cannot amend, distribute, sell, use, quote or paraphrase any part, or the content within this book, without the consent of the author or publisher.

Disclaimer Notice:

Please note the information contained within this document is for educational and entertainment purposes only. All effort has been executed to present accurate, up to date, and reliable, complete information. No warranties of any kind are declared or implied. Readers acknowledge that the author is not engaging in the rendering of legal, financial, medical or professional advice. The content within this book has been derived from various sources. Please consult a licensed professional before attempting any techniques outlined in this book.

By reading this document, the reader agrees that under no circumstances is the author responsible for any losses, direct or indirect, which are incurred as a result of the use of information contained within this document, including, but not limited to, — errors, omissions, or inaccuracies.

# Table of Contents

Introduction ................................................................................ 1

**Chapter 1: Introduction to the Industry** ................................ 3

    Exchange-Traded Funds ........................................................ 5

    Hedge Funds .......................................................................... 5

    Mutual Funds ......................................................................... 5

    Index Funds ........................................................................... 6

    Trust Funds ............................................................................ 6

    Asset Allocation ..................................................................... 7

    Portfolio Managers ............................................................... 7

    Investment Mandate ............................................................ 7

    Registered Investment Advisor ............................................ 7

    Stockbroker ........................................................................... 8

    Traditional IRA ...................................................................... 8

    401(k) ..................................................................................... 9

    Rollover IRA .......................................................................... 9

    Roth IRA ................................................................................ 9

    Closed-End .......................................................................... 11

    Open-End ............................................................................ 11

**Chapter 2: History of Mutual Funds** ............................................. **13**

**Chapter 3: What are Mutual Funds?** ........................................... **19**
    Liquidity ............................................................................... 21
    Professional Managers ........................................................ 21
    Mutual Fund Fees ................................................................ 22
    Tax Considerations .............................................................. 22
    Definition Of Closed-End Funds............................................ 24
    The Way Closed-End Fund Works ....................................... 25
    The Definition Of Open-End Funds....................................... 26
    The Way Open-End Funds Work ......................................... 27
    What Is Load Vs. No-Load? ................................................. 29
    Load Mutual Fund................................................................. 29
    No-Load Mutual Fund........................................................... 30

**Chapter 4: Benefits and Drawbacks of Mutual Funds**................**32**
    Benefits of Mutual Funds ..................................................... 33
    Drawbacks of Mutual Funds................................................. 35

**Chapter 5: Types of Mutual Funds** ............................................. **39**
    Money Market Funds ........................................................... 40
    Fund-of-Funds ..................................................................... 40
    Income Funds ...................................................................... 41
    Balanced Funds................................................................... 41
    Bond Funds ......................................................................... 41
    Equity Funds ....................................................................... 42
    International Funds .............................................................. 42
    Specialty Funds................................................................... 43

Socially-Responsible Funds.......................................................... 43
Index Funds.................................................................................. 44
Exchange Traded Funds (ETFs) ................................................... 44

## Chapter 6: The Traps Related to Mutual Funds .......................... 46
The Volume of Information ....................................................... 47
Market Reaction ........................................................................ 48
The Right Resource ................................................................... 48
Available Choices ...................................................................... 49
Part of Advertising .................................................................... 50
You'll Come Across Fees That Can Be Avoided ........................ 51
You Don't Have To Bear Sales Charges..................................... 51
You Believe That It Lacks Liquidity ........................................... 52
An Assumption On Annual Capital Gains Distributions............ 52

## Chapter 7: Detailed Information on the Mutual Fund Manager. 54
Duty of Hiring............................................................................ 58
Focusing on the Fund's Performance and Growth................... 58
Handling the Wealth ................................................................. 59
Accordance with Regulatory Authorities ................................. 60
Completing the Reporting Duties ............................................. 60
Successful Fund Managers ....................................................... 62

## Chapter 8: What Are Your Investment Goals?............................ 64
Risk Tolerance........................................................................... 65
Time Horizon ............................................................................ 66
Liquidity .................................................................................... 67
Reason for Investing ................................................................. 69

Realistic Ideas ................................................................... 70
Break it Into Chunks ......................................................... 70
Begin with Simple Things.................................................. 71

## Chapter 9: How to Manage Your Investment?.......................72

Begin Right Now ............................................................... 72
Focus on Diversification.................................................... 73
Name of the Fund ............................................................. 74
Market-Timing Strategy.................................................... 75
Wing-It Strategy................................................................ 75
Buy-and-Hold Strategy ..................................................... 76
Performance-Weighting Strategy..................................... 76

## Chapter 10: What Are Your Investment Strategies?...................81

1. Think about active or passive management................ 81
2. Budget calculation ...................................................... 82
3. The place to purchase mutual funds .......................... 83
4. Understanding the fees and charges.......................... 84
5. Create and manage the portfolio ............................... 85
   *Ways to manage investment risk ............................................ 86*
   *Invest in diversified equity schemes ........................................ 86*
   *Risk tolerance level ................................................................. 87*
   *Two main risk indicators.......................................................... 88*

## Chapter 11: Selecting and Utilizing the Mutual Fund .................91

Focus on The Fund Type and The Style ........................... 92
Check The Fees and Charges ............................................ 93
Get Clear About Past Results and Portfolio Managers............. 94

Think About The Things That Matter ............................................. 95
Avoid These Mistakes When Selecting Mutual Funds ............. 97
Researching On Past Performances ........................................... 97
Not Focusing On Tax Implications ............................................. 98
Overpaying Fees ........................................................................... 98
Not Being Considerate About Overlapping Investments ......... 98

## Chapter 12: Ways To Analyze Your Fund Performance ............ 100
Appropriate Benchmarks And Funds....................................... 100
Differentiate Good Performance That Might Turn Otherwise 101
Focus On The Economic Cycles................................................ 102
Find The Manager Tenure ........................................................ 102
Know About Expense Ratio ...................................................... 103
Think About The 5 And 10-Year Periods Of Performance...... 104
Research Sites For Mutual Funds ............................................ 105

## Chapter 13: Does Mutual Fund Investment Suit You? ............... 109
Mutual Funds vs. Stocks ........................................................... 113
Consider The Expenses And Fees ............................................ 114
Think About The Risk-Return .................................................. 115
Be Aware Of The Availability ................................................... 115

## Chapter 14: Practical Advice on Building Your Portfolio ........... 117
Think About The Core And Satellite Portfolio Design ............ 118
Don't Forget About Asset Allocation ....................................... 119
Keep In Mind Your Risk Tolerance Level ................................. 120
Dictate Your Investment Goals................................................ 120
Build Your Investment Style .................................................... 121

Learn To Diversify ............................................................. 121

## Chapter 15: FAQs on Mutual Funds ........................................ 123

What are mutual funds? ........................................................ 123

What do mutual funds invest in? .......................................... 123

What are the possible ways to make money? ..................... 124

What should be the fund's goal? .......................................... 124

What should be your mutual fund objectives? ................... 124

Do you think mutual funds are safe to invest? ................... 125

Why should you consider mutual fund investing? ............. 125

Who will manage your funds? .............................................. 126

What makes mutual fund investing a good choice? .......... 126

What are the options offered by a mutual fund? ............... 127

What does Redemption Price mean? ................................... 127

What does Exit Load mean? .................................................. 127

What is switching in a mutual fund? ................................... 127

Is there a fund that doesn't pay a dividend? ...................... 127

Do you know about the investment policy? ....................... 128

What is mutual fund liquidity? ............................................. 128

If a fund had positive returns, will it be the same this year too? ........................................................................ 128

Are Mutual Fund Investments risky? .................................... 129

What does a prospectus mean? ........................................... 129

How will you select the right mutual fund? ....................... 129

How can you compare the returns (rate) between different funds? ...................................................................... 130

Should retired people consider funds? ............................... 130

Where can you get advice regarding investing
    in mutual funds?................................................................ 130
Who should consider Mutual Funds?..................................... 131
How will you start investing in funds? ................................... 131

**Conclusion** ................................................................................. 133

**Reference** ................................................................................. 135

# Introduction

Most people invest blindly without knowing what investing really is! Do you know what it is? Probably, you don't! The reason you are reading this eBook is to gather knowledge on the subject of investing, to be more specific, a mutual fund. I know you probably have heard the term so many times, but it is high time you get into the subject to understand it. If you are considering mutual fund investing, it is essential to understand it clearly.

We all want to make money, and it is always about making *more* money. However, we are very much aware that it is not easy to make money. Remember, through proper investment you can cultivate the right system to gain a steady income. When it comes to investing, you must be vigilant in picking the right one. Although, it can be hard as there are so many choices that you can select from.

Even if there are so many choices, you can become bias towards one of the best investment methods; one investment is called mutual funds, and we are going to uncover the complete picture of a mutual fund investment in this eBook. I know it is impossible to learn everything related to mutual funds in one book, but you can get the required knowledge to kick-start your investing journey.

A mutual fund is great because it happens collectively. Investors securities are pooled together when dealing with a mutual fund. It is operated by professionals, so they bring income for the investors. Likewise, there are so many great benefits that you are going to learn from this book.

No journey is comfortable when you are just starting, thus don't believe mutual fund investing would be easy. If you want to make mutual fund investing a successful source of income, you must do the necessary requirements to make it one. You must make an effort to learn about mutual funding if you really want to get the best out of it! I'll make learning easy by compiling the basic information required for a beginner. Read the guide and get started!

Happy reading!

# Chapter 1

## Introduction to the Industry

You can begin your journey without considering the introduction of the mutual fund investing industry. If you are lucky enough, you'd be able to manage yourself even without understanding the introduction. When you are dealing with the investment industry, is it practical to rely on luck? I don't think it is vigilant to rely on luck if you aim to become a successful investor. Most people assume that finding a way to gain better income is all about finding a way to *get* better income. Yes, it is true. You have to find a way to get a better income but finding an approach will not suffice. Once you find a way to get a steady income, you must invest your time to learn about it. Having a complete understanding of the selected option is essential. Here we are discussing mutual fund investing. If you want to make a positive income you must learn it.

Most beginners think learning means reading a few blogs and articles. Well, education doesn't mean reading a few articles and blogs; you must get a clear picture of what mutual fund investing means. To do this, you must start by understanding the introduction to the industry. Sometimes, you might think that learning about mutual fund investing is a waste of time, but it is not! If you have a clear picture of mutual fund investments, you will be able to avoid a lot of problems that you might have to face otherwise. Presently, mutual fund investing is receiving a lot of recognition, and people are turning towards it to meet their financial goals. If you want to meet your financial goals, then this is a good choice. Let me help you by providing the required information on mutual fund investing.

Before we learn about mutual fund investing, it is important to know the investment structures available in the industry. You already know the reason why you must learn the investment structures. It is always better to know more than to know nothing.

There are different investment structures, so let's learn some of them below:

## Exchange-Traded Funds

You may have heard of ETFs, but it is okay if you haven't. ETFs are more like mutual funds, but they can be traded without any time limits like stocks. You have the opportunity to pay less or more than the underlying value of the fund holdings. There are situations where you'll be able to enjoy the tax advantages when dealing with ETFs.

## Hedge Funds

If you have come across investment partnerships, know that hedge funds belong to that category. Limited Liability Company or limited partnership are the regular listing options of hedge funds. The partners together perform extraordinary investing activities by pooling in their money. As you are a beginner, it is better to take some time before considering hedge funds because it is a bit risky when compared to typical investments. Leverage might be interesting, but it is not easy to tackle if you don't have enough experience. As a beginner, you must learn before you give it a go.

## Mutual Funds

Mutual funds are the most important investment structure and we'll be unfolding details about it throughout this eBook. However, it is better to touch every section of the industry, so you will have a clear idea about the overall industry. Mutual fund means pooling in money from many investors. The professional manager will handle the money while the investors purchase units or shares. A mutual fund is great because it saves your time and energy as you don't have to research when buying shares of companies. Like I mentioned earlier, the difference between ETFs and mutual fund is that a mutual fund is not traded without a time limit. The reason is investors will try to reap out benefits from the differences in the net asset value. Thus, investing orders are together executed after closing the markets. The final value of the day will be considered when executing the orders.

**Index Funds**

If you don't want to spend a lot of time researching or handling investment portfolios, you can consider index funds. This belongs to mutual funds and considered as an ETF at times. As an investor, you can invest in it, for example, the S&P 500 can be the index that you are investing in. You will be able to enjoy the returns that mirror the index. When dealing with index funds, managers will not focus on competition. Thus, it can be considered a great choice for passive investing. You don't have to bear a lot of costs as index funds are lower in expense ratio. Like I mentioned, you can consider index funds if you want a simple and straightforward investment option.

**Trust Funds**

This is a legal entity that helps a person save the assets that will be transferred to another individual or organization. There are different ways to hold assets in trust funds. Also, you can enjoy excellent protection, tax benefits, and much more. It is possible to hold stocks, real estate, bonds, hedge funds or mutual funds in trust funds. Basically, all the assets can be held in trust funds. You don't have to be wealthy to use trust funds. Instead, you have to be intelligent to use trust funds.

**Asset Allocation**

This is a framework used for asset classes. Generally, asset classes have different behavior patterns and characteristics. With the help of asset allocation, it is possible to find an investor's situation through which the rate of success will increase.

**Portfolio Managers**

They are experienced individuals who manage portfolios for investors. They group together assets and help the investors gain profit from them.

**Investment Mandate**

Rules, guidelines, and objectives are important, so investment mandate includes all these to handle a portfolio.

**Registered Investment Advisor**

This is a firm that provides advice, compensation, recommendations, security analyses, and issues reports. The firm helps through publications or directly. This firm may include investment advisory companies, asset management companies, and financial planning companies. The fiduciary duty is followed by RIAs, and it make things great for clients. The advisor fees will vary and definitely should be reasonable.

**Stockbroker**
A stockbroker can be an individual or an institution that trades on a customer's behalf. The duties of a stockbroker are settling trades, receives security, handles cash, and much more. You can get the support of a stockbroker for different stock trades, yet it is better not to rely too much on them.

These are some of the important factors that you need to know if you are beginning your journey as an investor. Of course, some information might not be directly related to mutual fund investing, yet they are important to be understood. Once you enter the investment industry, you'll be exposed to a lot of opportunities, and down the road, you might even widen your path. You might reach out to other investment opportunities, so it is a path for the ones who look forward to growing. Let's get into a few retirement accounts before detailing out mutual fund investment:

**Traditional IRA**
This is the oldest IRA that you will come across. It is a must to meet a few qualifications if you want to pour your money into it. Some of the investment types do not require investors to pay taxes.

**401(k)**

This is a special retirement plan offered to the employees. The 401(k) retirement plan lets the investor invest in mutual funds. Gaining tax deduction during the stage of funding is possible, but the annual limits are higher when compared to Roth IRA or traditional IRA. Basically, no taxes are involved until you withdraw at the age of 59.5 years and the essential distribution starts at the age of 70.5 years. Recently, investors have been given the opportunity to buy bonds and individual stocks. Also, note that 403(b) is another retirement plan that is offered by non-profit organizations and it is quite similar to a 401(k).

**Rollover IRA**

This is when the employee quits working or leaves the employer. In this case, the 401(k) can be shifted into a Rollover IRA. It happens by depositing the balance of 401(k) into this account.

**Roth IRA**

This is another special account based on the custody account, and through this special account, one can enjoy a lot of tax benefits. There are a few restrictions including the investment type and amount contributed. The money provided for Roth IRA will not be subjected to the tax deduction. Nevertheless, if you abide by the rules, you wouldn't have to pay taxes on the profits gained from the investment in Roth IRA. In fact, you don't have to handle taxes when withdrawing the profits.

These are the important retirement plans that you must know of. Now that you have entered into the industry, it is time to take the very first step. So, what actually is a mutual fund? Do you know about it or do you have zero knowledge about it? It doesn't matter even if you don't know about mutual funds because you'll be learning from scratch. I'll be covering another chapter that gives all the details on mutual funds clearly and perfectly. Anyway, let's get some understanding of mutual funds. This is one of the methods to build wealth, especially for the newcomers of the investment industry.

We discussed retirement plans like 401(k) and IRA because you can deal with mutual funds through such plans as well. If you don't prefer retirement plans, you can consider the brokerage account. But to consider any of these, you must know how mutual funds work, how to invest mutual funds, and many other crucial factors. If you ask me, I'd say as a beginner you must consider mutual funds, not because this eBook is specifically about it but because it is easy. You don't have to stress a lot when you are handling mutual funds. If you compare other investment options, apparently, you'd have to deal with high-stress levels. Yes, it is pooling in money from investors, but you should not dive in without learning how to swim in this market.

The mutual fund investment collects all the money offered by companies, organizations, and investors. The money collected will be handled and managed by the fund manager. But there'll be a specific goal for the fund manager, and it varies as per the fund type. For example, if it is a manger related to fixed-income, he or she will be focusing on the lowest risk and highest yield that can be offered to an investor. You will be learning about mutual fund managers in the following chapters. The mutual funds divide into two main types such as closed-end funds and open-end funds. Here's a brief explanation of each type:

**Closed-End**

The closed-end fund deals with a specific number of shares while being traded on the open market. The specific number of shares will be offered to the general public in an initial offering. You must also know that the closed-end fund will not issue more shares or redeem like the usual mutual fund. Due to supply and demand factors, the shares are traded at a discount net asset value.

**Open-End**

The open-end fund deals with the highest percentage of mutual funds. Basically, there is no specific number of shares in the open-end fund. Even though there is no specific number of shares, the new shares issued under this category will be on the current net asset value. Also, the investor will be requested to redeem the shares if he or she decides to sell. The shares under this category will deal with a net asset value of the underlying investments because producing and destroying shares will happen as per the requirements.

However, that's not all. You have a lot to learn about mutual fund investing, and I'll be helping you learn all the essential details.

Beginners often fail even though mutual fund investing is one of the most comfortable investment options. Why? They think they'll manage it just because it is considered easy, even so, as a beginner you have to do your part. Your part is to educate yourself about mutual fund investing!

## Chapter 2

## History of Mutual Funds

You might have thought that mutual fund investing is super easy so you can get started right away. Yes, it is super easy, but it doesn't mean you can skip learning the history of mutual funds. Do you know how important history is? By learning the history of mutual funds, you will get a clear view about the investment method. You will understand how it all started. Maybe you have selected mutual fund investing due to its simplicity. If you are investing in mutual funds you don't have to spend a lot of time to build your portfolio and it is one of the main reasons people turn towards it.

The investment intermediary is when the investors pool in money as per their objectives. The proportionate amount received by the investor will be decided upon the initial investment. The objective of the investment should be pre-determined. The mutual funds deal with stocks, bonds, real estate, money-market instruments, and commodities. As a beginner, you must ensure to check the fund's prospectus before beginning your journey as it will contain important factors such as objectives, funds' policies, service, and charges. Every investor must know all these factors if they want to invest successfully.

There are different risk levels for various funds. For example, compare the risk rate of government bond investments and stock investments, you will understand that the risk rate is greater for a stock investment than a government bond. Thus, it is important to focus on the risk's levels related to different funds. Likewise, there are a lot of factors that you need to understand about mutual funds. But let's leave the facts pertaining to mutual funds here and discuss them in the following chapters. Now, it's time to learn the history of mutual funds.

Many historians are not certain about the start of investment funds. In the 18th or 19th century, pooling of assets started in the Netherlands, but it was also mentioned based on some indications.

Closed-end funds started to become famous in the 1800s in France and Great Britain. In the 1890s, it started moving towards the United States. In 1924, Massachusetts Investors' Trust was created in Boston, and in 1928 it was made public. In the same year, the United States got access to mutual funds. By 1929, the competition between closed-end and open-end funds was high. It was the competition between 19 open-end funds vs. 700 closed-end funds. However, the market crash that happened in 1929 made things worse for closed-end funds. A large amount of highly leveraged funds (closed-end) got wiped out. Yet, a few open-end funds remained in the market.

It was clear that the safety of investments will not be guaranteed unless for the Securities and Exchange Commission (SEC). As per the Investment Company Act of 1940 and Securities Act of 1934 the SEC is regulated safeguard mutual fund investments. The mutual fund gradually got popular for two decades since the 1950s. The bull market popularity and growth increased in the 1980s and 1990s which created over $1 trillion total assets and fund over 3,000 in this period. The mutual fund investment was a growing market even in 2006, and the United States asset holdings were more than $10.4 trillion. In fact, many new markets opened up in every part of the world.

In the 1980s and 1990s mutual funds gained public interest. Investors received incredible returns during this period. Even though mutual fund investment started in Netherland, the growth and popularity of it have reached the top. Now, it is an international industry, and the United States alone handles more than trillions of dollars. You wouldn't have assumed that mutual fund investments would have an interesting history like this. Moreover, the history of mutual fund investing is pretty fun and interesting, so let's continue.

King William I launched a few investment companies related to mutual funds in 1822 in the Netherlands. There are details that say that a trust investment was made in Dutch merchant, Adriaan van Ketwich's name; it was created in 1744 and would have given the idea regarding mutual funds. Van Ketwich's theory focuses on diversifying as it will enhance the chances for investments with minimum capital. Van Ketwich's fund means "unity creates strength." In 1849, many other similar mutual funds were added to the trust in Switzerland and in 1880, Scotland had investment opportunities as well.

After mutual funds got introduced in the United States in 1893, the Boston Personal Property Trust was formed. It was the initial closed-end fund that was formed in the United States. After, the modern mutual fund came into the picture. After introducing Alexander Fund in 1907 in Philadelphia, there was a drastic positive change in the mutual fund industry. It was the evolutionary step towards the modern mutual fund.

That was the beginning of modern mutual fund, and the indication was in 1928 for the arrival of the modern mutual fund. The investors also were given access to a mutual fund that year. Over time, the MFS investment management firm was opened. Even the State Street Investors' Trust wasn't operating on its own, and rather it was treated as Massachusetts Investors' Trust custodian. But later in 1924, State Street Investors' Trust made its own firm with Richard Saltonstall, Paul Cabot, and Richard Paine. The first no-load fund was launched in 1928. In the same year, the Wellington Fund was launched as well. Wellington Fund was the initial fund to add bonds and stocks. Hence, this was a significant period when discussing the mutual fund. In fact, the industry was booming in the 1960s and was supporting the bear market in 1969 to provide access to the public. Yet, over time the growth of the industry wasn't booming anymore.

However, there were a few developments in 1971. First of all, John McQuown and William Fouse introduced the initial index fund. In the 1970s the no-load fund was introduced. This introduction had a new and positive impact on the industry. Right after the bull market introduction, the fund managers played the best part. Peter Lynch, Michael Price, and Max Heine were the top market players. The inflow of cash was happening at a high rate. All the good things ended and sacred the majority in 2007; the great recession happened. During this period, the financial crisis was high in the whole world.

In spite of the financial crisis in 2007 and the 2003 scandals, the mutual fund industry never stopped growing. In the United States itself there are 10,000 plus mutual funds, and it is still growing. Even after the introductions of separate accounts, competing products, and ETFs, the industry of mutual funds continued to grow successfully. Retail investors' backbone is nothing but mutual funds, and it will be a means to many newcomers as well. [1]

As you already know, history is essential. If you know history, you will be able to understand how everything started. Most beginners think learning history is not something fundamental so spending time on it will only reduce your time that you can otherwise allocate for essential things.

Remember, earning high returns should be your goal, but it shouldn't be your ONLY goal. If you get attracted to profits and growth, you will not think about the ways to achieve them. Instead, you will try to gain profits and growth without any actual process. But it will not help you make a good income unless you know the process. To know the process, you must start from the history of mutual funds.

---

[1] Mcwhinney, J. (2018) A Brief History of the Mutual Fund.

# Chapter 3

# What are Mutual Funds?

A mutual fund portfolio can't be recreated on your own; thus, the support of portfolio managers is crucial. Most beginners fail to understand the importance of a manager's role, yet the manager's part is very much needed. Mutual funds are one of the excellent investment strategies that an investor must consider. The net asset value (NAV) is the price of mutual funds. The NAV is decided by dividing the total securities' value by a fund's outstanding shares. The value of securities that remain in the portfolio when a business day ends will have a clear impact on the NAV. You must understand that you don't own the security that you invested in. Instead, you own the shares.

Most of the time, actively managed funds will be different. How? The decisions related to actively managed funds will be decided by the portfolio managers along with the support of researchers. If you look at a portfolio manager's main goal, it would be to find opportunities that support to outperform the benchmarks of the fund. You can settle for a fund manager based on the returns gained in relation to the benchmark of the fund. Perhaps, you might look for short-term goals and performance when selecting a fund. But remember, it is always better to have ideas and thoughts about long-term performances.

A beginner's first choice should be mutual funds because it is cost-effective and smart. You don't have to worry about the minimum purchase because it can be decided on your own and you don't have to adhere to any rules. Also, note that there are chances for you to enjoy reductions if you purchase funds using brokerage features or through a retirement account. It is highly risky when you have all the investments in one basket, thus diversifying is a great choice. The mutual fund helps you to diversify the investments, so you don't have to handle high risks. There are cases where mutual funds hold more than 100 securities. However, as a beginner, there are many factors that you must know so let's learn some of those briefly.

## Liquidity

It is important to understand liquidity to know how convenient mutual funds are! If you are buying or selling fund shares, you are given the opportunity to do it throughout the day. You not only have the liberty to invest throughout the day but also to contribute for additional investments such as capital gain and dividend reinvestment at any preferred time. The initial investment required for stock funds is lower than the requirement for individual stocks. Perhaps, nobody likes to pick the complex choice, so it is apparent that you'd pick the most convenient investment option.

## Professional Managers

A professional manager can be a great benefit for you. As an investor (mutual fund), you get to enjoy the services of a professional manager. The manager will review your portfolio from time to time to ensure that everything is alright. The analysts and the portfolio managers are experts in their field, so you don't have to worry about obtaining their services. They even possess the required technology resources that are essential for research and analysis regarding the marker and investments. They help you make the right investment decision through their analysis. The fund manager's duty is to focus on the security evaluation and sector allocation. There are technical factors that are used in this process, and the manager will utilize it perfectly while helping you to identify the right security to buy or sell. If you don't have enough time or expertise regarding mutual fund investing, professional managers must be your pillar of support.

## Mutual Fund Fees

You can easily overlook a few factors and say that you did it to save time. But remember, as a beginner, you definitely need to learn all these factors as they will help you make clear decisions. One factor overlooked by most beginners is mutual fund fees. First of all, you must understand that there are different fees when dealing with mutual funds. Thus, trying to learn them will not be a waste. Certain funds have transaction charges when buying and selling. Sometimes, you'd have to deal with commissions and loads. You might have to bear a redemption fee when you sell shares that are owned only for some time. There will be ongoing expenses as well: costs of operating, investment advisory fee, and transaction cost. You must not forget about the fees when you are evaluating funds because it impacts the performance. It is important to consider mutual fund fees when you are dealing with mutual funds.

## Tax Considerations

You'll receive interest or dividends from the securities in the portfolio. The fund manager gets the opportunity to sell securities after value increment. The investor will receive income from these events, but as for law, it should be paid in a periodic distribution format. During this distribution, you'll have to bear taxes if you own shares in the fund. The federal exemption is available for the income received from municipal bonds investment. Also, if you are not investing through IRA or any other tax-beneficiary accounts, you'll have to handle three types of taxes:

1. Your dividend income will be taxed (regular income tax rate).

2. Your capital gains obtained by selling securities will be taxed (regular income tax rate or based on long-term capital gains rate).

3. Your capital gains obtained by exchanging or selling shares with a profit will be taxed (regular income tax rate or based on long-term capital gains rate).

So that's all the basic details you need to know about mutual funds. If you don't know the basic factors, you will struggle a lot down the road. Instead, it is better to spend time to learn the market before actually investing in it. Once you have learned the basic factors, you must focus on the closed-end and open-end funds. I have given a brief explanation in chapter 1, but now let's study the elaborated information on these types.

The difference between closed-end and open-end funds

At the beginning of your journey, mutual funds may look complicated than you may have thought. Most of the time, complicated things produce better results. Even if mutual funds are complicating right now, over time, you will find it easier. In fact, through learning and practice, there's nothing that can't be achieved.

That said, even mutual funds will be easy if you learn it in-depth. If you are planning to invest in mutual funds, it is important to understand the difference between these two funds.

You might consider open-end funds as a safer selection when compared to closed-end funds. But if you look at the returns, you will gain better returns from the closed-end fund because of the capital appreciation and dividend payment. When you are making a decision, you must compare and contrast the choices available, so that you will better understand.

**Definition Of Closed-End Funds**

A closed-end fund is an investment model that issues only a specific number of shares that you can't redeem from it. New shares will not be created by the manager when dealing with closed-end funds. If you know how ETFs work, you can easily understand CEFs because they work quite alike. Initial Public Offering (IPO) launching is done to increase the value and then, traded just like ETFs or stocks in the open market. You must not forget the fact that it is valued as per NAV. Even though the share value will be based on NAV, supply and demand will affect the price. Thus, one can trade below or above the actual value. In 2017, the market held above $275 billion closed-end funds. You must understand that closed-end funds use leverage to make higher gains. Even though investing the money borrowed can be dangerous, you'll still make higher returns.

## The Way Closed-End Fund Works

A management team and investment advisors handle the closed-end and open-end funds. Closed-End funds help to make capital gain distributions and you'd have to bear an annual expense. However, Securities and Exchange Commission registration is required for the fund and the portfolio manager. Closed-End funds are actively managed when compared to index mutual funds and ETFs. Even the portfolio of securities will be focused on the geographic market or specific industry.

There are clear differences between closed-end funds and open-end funds. There are fundamental ways of how closed-end and open-end funds differ. The fund raised by closed-end fund will be a one-time thing done through IPO. A certain number of shares will be offered to investors to purchase. Once the set number of shares are sold, the offering will be closed, and now, you know why it is a closed-end fund. After closing the offering, there will not be any new investment in it. On the other hand, ETFs and mutual funds issue additional shares, add new investor dollars, and redeem shares.

The stock exchange list will have closed-end funds shares to be traded throughout the day. But the clear cut difference is that open-end funds can't be traded throughout the day like closed-end funds. Instead, it will be at the end of the day. Even the NAV will differ as per the market forces (supply and demand, change in values of securities) if it's a closed-end fund. Also, remember, a brokerage account is required if you are buying and selling closed-end funds. If it was an open-end fund, it is possible to purchase directly.

Before we move on to open-end funds, let's check out the benefits and drawbacks of closed-end funds.

The benefits of a closed-end fund are:

- Diversified portfolios
- Transparent pricing
- Professional management
- Better yields

The drawbacks of a closed-end fund are:

- Volatility
- The requirements for brokers
- Less liquidity
- Heavily discounted

## The Definition Of Open-End Funds

Among the two types of funds, now let's understand about open-end funds. This is what you consider a mutual fund. There is no limit in regard to sharing issues. When investors buy shares in mutual funds, it will not limit to the purchase. Rather, more shares will be created. Once an investor sells shares, those shares will be removed from circulation. When there is redemption, the investor must be paid, and for that, the mutual fund must sell some investments. There is no chance for you to watch open-end funds like you do with stocks as it can't be traded on the open market. At the end of the day, the re-pricing will be done based on shares sold and bought. I've already mentioned the way NAV is calculated. Now, let's see how the open-end fund works.

**The Way Open-End Funds Work**
The open-end fund will issue shares as per the buyer's request. It is an open investment, and that is where an open-end fund gets its name. When shares are purchased from the fund, it will be a path to create more shares. But when shares are sold, it will be removed from circulating. Basically, the purchasing and selling of shares will be based on NAV. The open-end fund offers investors an easy way to kick-start their investing journey. It is one of the best ways to have a diversified portfolio to meet your investment goals. If you want a low-cost method, this can be the best option that you must consider.

Your investing objectives can be income, growth, and much more. Also, target investments can be any specific industry. You don't normally need a huge amount to access an open-end fund. Thus, it is accessible for investors at any level. Once the management decides that the total assets in the fund are large enough to be executed, the new investors will not be able to access the fund. As a beginner, you must understand the details in-depth because if not you'd have a hard time achieving your financial goals.

You must also consider the benefits and drawbacks related to open-end funds.

The benefits of an open-fund are:

- Less risk due to diversified portfolios
- Highly liquid
- Professional money management
- Low investment minimums

The drawbacks of an open-end fund are:

- Priced only once in a day
- Require high cash reserves
- Lower yields
- High expenses and fees

No you have some level of understanding about both closed-end and open-end funds. However, you must understand that learning should not stop here. Instead, you must learn as much as you can. You must search for information from reliable sources. Most beginners do not want to spend their time learning, but remember, it is part of your journey. Now, let's get started on another section of mutual funds that you must be aware of: Load vs. No-load, do you know what they are? Let's see!

## What Is Load Vs. No-Load?

The charges and the fees are often considered as the base to categorize mutual funds. When we are speaking about fees and charges, it is important to know about sales charge, an example being load funds. On the other hand, funds that don't involve a sales charge are called no-load funds. The investors must consider loads as it is part of the fees. Of course, it is essential to pay the management professionals. Sometimes, there will be controversies with mutual funds fees, so you have to be mindful about it.

## Load Mutual Fund

Basically, the amount charged as for sales or commission when purchasing shares is what we call as load mutual fund. It will be a flat fee or a percentage as per your investment and the mutual fund provider. For example, if your investment amount is $500 and the load is 5% so that your actual investment amount would be $475. Thus, the rest $25 is the commission for the company. The fee will be for a broker, sales intermediary, investment advisor, or for a financial advisor. The payment is for investing their time and talent to select the right fund for you. As an investor, you'll come across a few types of load and here are they:

Class A shares also known as front-end loads, is a payment made by the investor when purchasing shares.

Class B shares also known as back-end loads, is a fee paid (one-time) when selling or redeeming shares.

Class C shares also known as level load funds, is a fixed annual charge collected as a percentage from the fund's asset.

Loads have an impact on the mutual funds of the investors. Certain loads will decrease the returns so that the final amount will be divided among the investors. You must understand that loads play an essential role, so ignoring it would be disadvantageous for you!

**No-Load Mutual Fund**

A no-load mutual fund is when the investor doesn't have to bear sale charges when selling or buying shares. But let me make it clear for you, even though there will not be sale charges it doesn't mean you'll not have ANY charges at all. Therefore, let's learn more about the no-load mutual fund.

The Financial Industry Regulatory Authority (FINRA) charges is about 12-1b. If a fund wants to focus on the no-load fund, the charges imposed by the fund should be less than the charges allowed by FINRA. Even though there will not be any back load or front load fees, you might have to deal with some other fees. You can read the prospectus to know about the charges. Any charges will be paid as per the daily NAV, and the management firm will handle it. This can be an issue for investors who gain smaller distribution.

If you are a short-term investor, you will have to bear a fee when you sell the shares early, but a long-term investor doesn't have to worry about this. Thus, you must know that no-load fund shares should be redeemed or sold within the described period. Basically, there are certain limitations in regard to redemption.

An investment company becomes the middleman when selling no-load funds so no sales firm would have a third party's interference. However, you might have to meet the demands of broker-dealers or banks.

There are different conclusions related to no-load and load mutual funds. But I'm not going to be biased towards any of these. I must provide information that will help you make a wise decision. As I've mentioned before, don't stick to one source, and keep looking for more information if you want to become a successful investor!

# Chapter 4

# Benefits and Drawbacks of Mutual Funds

Before you invest in a mutual fund, you must understand what mutual fund is! Learning the definition is the first step towards your investing journey. Once you have learned the benefits, you can move on to the next step, which is getting to know the benefits and drawbacks of mutual funds. Most beginners do not spend time to learn the benefits and drawbacks because they believe it is not essential. You shouldn't fall into that category; appreciate the time that you spend learning.

Of course, nobody can deny the fact that mutual funds are a great way to begin your investment journey because it is easy and cost-effective. You can enjoy professional management service, liquidity, and diversification through mutual funds. But remember, just like for everything else, you'd have to deal with certain costs. One of the costs is the charges imposed on the investors when they are buying or selling shares in the mutual funds. Just like this, there are many drawbacks related to mutual funds. But as a beginner, you shouldn't give up on mutual fund investing just because of the drawbacks. There are different ways to handle those drawbacks, so you must know what they are! Let's begin with the benefits.

## Benefits of Mutual Funds

*Professional management.* One of the best things about mutual funds is professional management. The managers in the team are experienced enough and well-trained. They will manage your funds accordingly. When you are purchasing mutual funds, there will be a management fee that you must bear. It will be a part of the expense ratio. The management fee is utilized to find a professional manager to handle your portfolio. The price you pay for the management will not be a waste because their help is tremendous.

*Instant diversification.* This is one of the reasons why people consider mutual funds. Diversifying your portfolio will help the investors to reduce risks and to achieve their financial goals. It is possible to own many shares in different corporations from a single investment. A portfolio will have a combination of stocks, commodities, and bonds. Basically, mutual funds are diversified. Even if a stock goes down, an investor doesn't have to worry because there are other assets to compensate. The potential loss will spread out, so you'll benefit that way and this benefit will be a means to risk reduction as well.

*Convenience.* If you compare other investments to mutual funds, you will understand that mutual funds are much easier and convenient. Even an average level investor can consider mutual funds because of its simplicity. Not only is it convenient but it is also easy to purchase and understand. For mutual funds, the minimum investment is around $2500 along with a one-time trading opportunity in a day at closing NAV. Thus, the simplest procedures to handle mutual funds make it a wonderful choice.

*Investment size.* Even if you don't have investing experience or financial management skills, you can still turn towards mutual funds. In fact, the investment size is not too large, which makes it possible for an investor to invest in mutual funds even if he or she has a small amount.

*Liquidity.* One of the essential factors that deal with mutual funds is its liquidity. Say you want to quit investing in a mutual fund; you don't have to complicate the process. Why? You can easily inform your financial advisor or your broker about it. By doing this, they will sell it right away, and that's it. Your funds will be back to your account in a day, unlike individual stocks that takes a longer time to liquidate. Therefore, liquidity is another reason why you must consider mutual funds.

*Your style.* Yes, you can find funds that suit your style. You might have certain expectations from an investment. Thus, you can find funds to meet your needs.

*Dividend Reinvestment.* This is a great method to grow your investment, and this is one of the benefits that you can get from mutual funds. The interest income and dividends can be used in order to buy more shares and an example of this is reinvesting.

## Drawbacks of Mutual Funds

*Management Fees.* The companies must pay marketing expenses and salaries, and it should be before paying the investors. The management fees are one of the drawbacks because it has the power to eat your profits even without you knowing it. Thus, you have to be careful about management fees. Don't imagine that higher fees equal better performance because it doesn't happen that way. However, you have to be clear and vigilant when you are dealing with management fees.

*The type.* Obviously, as a beginner, you will not be aware of the type of mutual funds. So, what should you do? It is pretty simple, and you should seek advice from a financial advisor. If you are clear about your financial goals, you can easily settle for the right type of investment. But if you don't, you will have a hard time finding the right investment type.

*Cash payment.* Often, people withdraw mutual funds. Hence, cash balances are important. When paying in cash, there will not be any interests collected for you. This might be a bother to some people.

*Mutual Fund Charges.* This happens when an investor redeems money. Not only will this happen, but you might also come across operating expenses, and it differs as per the investment amount. As a beginner, you must not overlook sales and expense ratios because if you don't consider it, the damage can be huge. You must be cautious when you are investing with 1.2% or higher expense ratios. Like I explained before, you can find companies with no sales charges. Yet, the choice is yours, and when selecting a particular company or a fund, you must do your research. Don't select blindly.

*Management abuses.* If your decision in selecting a manager is not accurate, you'd have to deal with window dressing, churning, and much more. You might have to handle excessive replacement, unnecessary trading, and much more. Thus, you must not let management abuse happen when you are handling mutual funds.

*Poor trade execution.* The same-day NAV is important to be understood because if you place a trade, the closing price will not make any changes to your decision when you purchase or sell a mutual fund. For someone who needs quick execution, the mutual fund execution strategy may not be beneficial. The mutual fund execution strategy centers upon day trading, short-term goals, and timing; thus, it is not possible.

*Tax inefficiency.* You can't avoid capital gain payouts when you are dealing with mutual funds. You might have to deal with uncontrollable tax events as well, so you have no choice in regard to taxation. This is one of the main drawbacks in mutual funds.

Sometimes, you might feel as if certain drawbacks are not actually drawbacks. Maybe some benefits do not actually benefit you. In such instances, you must make sure to do further research without concluding anything. However, as a beginner, once you know the drawbacks related to mutual funds, you will feel as if you don't want to enter into the mutual fund investing industry. But don't let it happen because you can handle drawbacks successfully if you understand why such drawbacks persist. You don't want to do this only with mutual fund investing, but with anything that you do for the first time because it will be a bit difficult. Therefore, don't let a few drawbacks stop you from reaching your goals.

With that being said, let me explain one of the important sections that bother every beginner. Which is better, individual stocks or mutual fund investing? Let's read to find out!

If you consider mutual fund investment over individual stocks, you can save some time that you would otherwise have to spend in researching. There will be different stocks in a mutual fund that are divided into small blocks. You already know that ETFs and mutual funds have been there for investors for quite some time. Naïve investors will be able to diversify your portfolio even without any research regarding the stocks and individual companies.

Even though many funds have done a great job in the market, around 90% of the funds were not able to beat a large number of U.S. stocks. Mutual funds are considered cost-effective, but if you don't analyze the fees and costs, you will have regret deciding to invest in mutual funds. Don't ignore the importance of learning the fees and costs related to mutual funds.

Most beginners believe that the stock market offers the best when you pay more. Basically, it is believed that with bigger returns there are bigger fees. Don't buy into this false notion; instead, the opposite is true. Most of the time, lower fees offer more significant returns. Of course, the stock market has no guarantee that you will gain profits. Not only the stock market, but none of the markets offers the guarantee for steady profit. Whatever you do, you must ensure that you understand the complete picture before making any decision. Also, you must not give up investing if you face losses the first time because losses are inevitable. In investing and trading, you will definitely face losses but you must strive for success. If you are not ready to handle risks, you must stay away from investing in mutual funds. If you believe that you can handle it and if you know how the financial system works, then it is okay to give it a try. Nevertheless, single stock investing is risky when compared to mutual fund investing.

Of course, there are a lot of opportunities in the world of investment. No matter your choice of investment, what you should do is to test the waters before you jump in. Take time and learn everything that you can. Find details about how the market operates and how you have to perform and so much more! If you want to succeed in mutual fund investing, you have to be confident and smart!

## Chapter 5

## Types of Mutual Funds

It is not enough to know the pros and cons and just enter the investing industry. There is a lot more than you think that goes into investing. For example, there are different types of mutual funds. When you enter the mutual fund industry, you might not have known or thought of the many types of mutual funds. However, it is essential to be aware of the types if you are planning to invest in mutual funds. As previously mentioned, no matter your style, there'll be a fund that matches your investing taste and goals.

It is apparent that mutual funds deal with risk and reward profiles. Typically, if the potential return is higher, the risk will be too. But you can't avoid the fact that certain funds will be riskier than others. When you are dealing with mutual funds, you must know that there will be risks at some level and you can never find funds that don't involve certain risks. Even if you stick to money market funds (there will be more on this later), you will still have risks to handle because that's how the industry works. Risk is a common factor in all types of investment and not only for mutual funds.

Every fund has its own investment objective that caters to the need of investors.

Before we dig deeper into the different types of funds, you should get to know the basic types such as equity funds, fixed-income funds, money-market funds, and balanced funds. These are the basic asset classes, and the funds that we are going to discuss will be parallel with these classes. However, let's begin learning these types of funds.

**Money Market Funds**
Earlier, I was talking about money market funds so now, let's discuss it in-depth. This is considered as the safest debt-instrument (short-term). These are considered risk-free as well and especially, Treasury bills offered by the government. This is an ideal spot to keep your money even though there will not be substantial returns. Yet, you won't be subjected to the loss of capital, which is great. The return would be a bit lower than the certificate of deposit (average) and a bit higher than a normal savings account. Even though money market funds are dealt with ultra-safe assets, the financial crisis in 2008 hit hard on the share price. So, that was an instance when money market funds were hit with losses.

**Fund-of-Funds**
This is when funds invest in some other funds, just like balanced funds. The simple reason behind this is to help the investors allocate assets and to simplify diversification. Marketing Expense Ratio for this type is higher than stand-alone funds.

## Income Funds

This fund is basically what the name suggests. A steady income will be provided to the investors. These are invested in quality corporate debt and in the government and until maturity, these bonds will be held as it will provide interest. Even though holding these funds will appreciate its value, the main goal is to create a steady income. Mostly, retirees and conservative investors will consider income funds as it focuses on a regular income. The ones who are conscious about tax will not consider income funds.

## Balanced Funds

Providing income, capital appreciation, and safety are the major objectives of these funds. The main strategy used by the balanced fund is to consider both equities and fixed income investment portfolios. There is a certain regular percentage for balanced fund weighting. It might be restricted as per the asset class limitations as well. There is another similar fund: asset allocation fund. Even though asset allocation funds have similar objectives, the specified percentage requirement is not applicable for this fund. The ratio of asset classes will be different as per the business cycle, and the portfolio manager will have the liberty to change accordingly.

## Bond Funds

Investors actively trade and invest bond funds. These funds are actively managed. In fact, investors look for undervalued bonds so that they sell them with a profit. Even though mutual funds have higher returns compared to money market investments, it is not the case with bonds. These funds come with risk. The reason is bonds vary, and they have different types. In fact, it varies as to where it is invested. However, you must not forget that bond funds deal with interest rate risks. Thus, if you want to consider bond funds make sure to collect more experience and knowledge about it.

**Equity Funds**

This is one of the most popular mutual funds in the market. Investing in stocks is the major concern of these funds. The objective is long-term growth (capital). One can't limit equity funds as one category because there are different types under these funds. The reason is there are different equities, so the types also vary.

**International Funds**

Foreign fund or international fund is just like the name suggests. These funds invest outside one's home country. It is not an easy task to say whether these funds are safer or riskier than the regular investments in one's home country, but it's apparent that they are volatile and risky when considering the political risks of a country. On the other hand, international funds can be a great support for a balanced portfolio because they reduce the risk through diversification. However, as a beginner, you must not directly pick this fund, but you can consider these funds once you become familiar with the market and investing.

## Specialty Funds

This is quite different from the ones we discussed above. The special funds consist of all the popular funds, but they are not rigid like the other funds. These funds refrain from broad diversification because they have a targeted strategy or a specific economic segment. A specialty fund like sector funds focus on sectors such as health, technology, financial, and more. Therefore, sector funds can be highly volatile because of the correlation between the stocks in the sector. Even though there is a high chance for greater gains, there are chances for huge losses as well. Likewise, the best thing about regional funds is that you can easily focus on the geographic area or a country. If you make an effort to learn and understand these funds, you will be able to buy stocks abroad. If you try otherwise, you'll have a hard time doing it. Also, it can be expensive. Like I said for sector funds, with regional funds you have to be ready for higher risks if the country's economy or the region faces a bad recession. It is better to learn in-depth before considering any of these funds.

## Socially-Responsible Funds

This is one of my absolute favorites because it is a socially responsible fund. The investors who invest in socially-responsible funds have certain criterions, so they invest in companies that match their criterion. They don't include "sin" industries to their list, such as nuclear power, alcoholic beverages, and tobacco. Their focus is on the competitive performance, but not by compromising their values. Usually, industries considered by these investors are industries that concentrate on recycling, solar power or wind power.

## Index Funds

These funds want to perform just like the Dow Jones Industrial Average (DJIA) and S&P 500. The investors who accept the fact that active portfolio managers will not be handle the market regularly will focus on index funds. The index funds involve low fees and replicate the returns, so they are the major benefits for the investors.

## Exchange Traded Funds (ETFs)

We've already discussed a little bit about ETFs. ETFs are one of the most popular investments in the market. The strategies used by ETFs are similar to the ones used for mutual funds. But these funds are considered as investment trusts and traded on the stock exchange. In fact, these funds are great because they have the stocks' features. For example, like stocks you can buy and sell ETFs at any time throughout the day. Even the fees are lower when compared to the mutual fund (equivalent fund) fees. Also, you can purchase ETFs or short sell on margin. The versatility is the main reason for the popularity of ETFs.

You must try to learn more about these funds because you can't win the market with limited knowledge and practice! In fact, it is hard to settle for a specific type of fund with limited knowledge. Sometimes, from the definition, you might feel as if it's the right choice. But once you dig deeper and find the pros and cons of each fund, you will feel that there's more to it. Thus, the best option is to learn the funds before making any decision! An informed decision will pave the path to a successful investment journey!

# Chapter 6

# The Traps Related to Mutual Funds

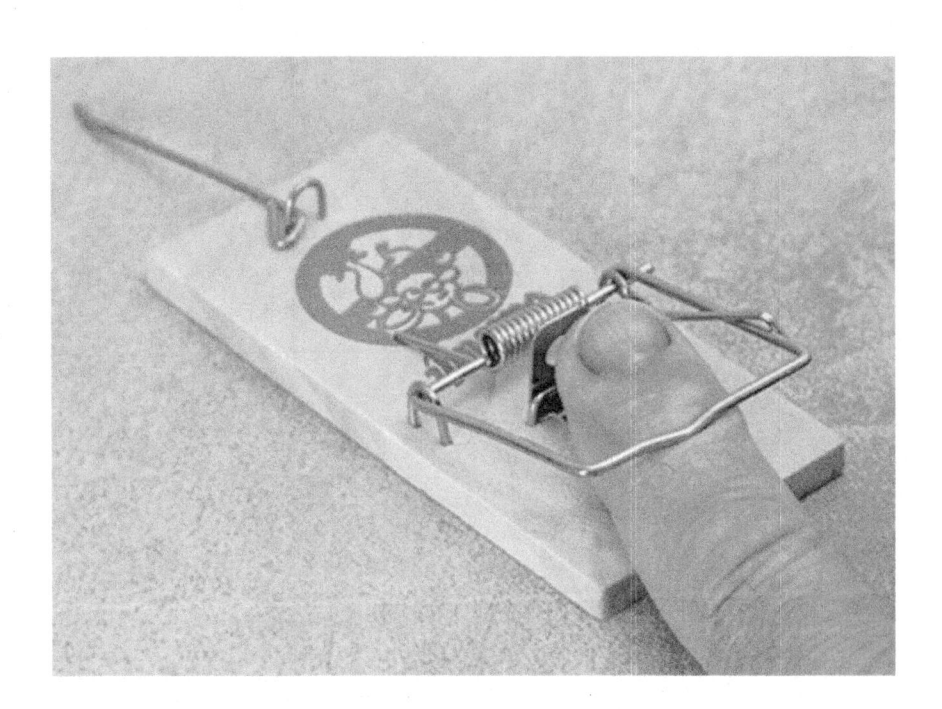

Before we learn the traps related to mutual funds, it is essential to understand the common problems people face when they enter the investing world. Why should you know this? As a beginner, it is highly possible for you to face these problems. Thus, it is better to know the problems beforehand. Sometimes, you might think that the time spent learning these basic details is a waste, well you might want to think twice about that. If you think you are wasting your time, you'd have to spend more time correcting them. Instead, it is better to enter the investing world with the right knowledge to fix these problems before they create conflict for you.

Most beginners think that the basics of investing has not changed for many years. Of course, the buying and selling concept has not changed. However, it doesn't mean that nothing is different. There are a few factors that investors must know about the modern investing industry. It is pretty obvious that there will be changes when the industry develops and evolves over time. Assuming that it will never change and remain the same, is not practical. So, here are some factors you should know:

**The Volume of Information**
Of course, no one can deny the fact that the volume of information is immense. Even though one may consider it as a benefit, it is not a benefit all the time. Perhaps modern investors struggle a lot with the volume of information available. Back then, solid information was available, so investors were not struggling to find reliable details. In fact, they did not have to handle the volume of information streaming in. Publicly traded companies tend to offer reports quarterly and annually. The finance publications were limited, so the business news and information were not coming from multiple sources. Even if the news or reports were to be considered, they must be verified, written, printed, and offered to the public.

Now, the way of informing the public has changed. Almost all companies produce information limitlessly. You might come across information related to daily price fluctuations, posts, and other messages related to investing from different sources. When information streams in, you will find it hard to select reliable information. There are different challenges that you will face when you are looking for information in this modern investing industry.

**Market Reaction**
Quality information is helpful, but what if the market doesn't react the way you want it to react? Even if there is enough information, you can still find problems when the market reaction is uncertain. Also, there is no limit for inaccurate information, and you don't have enough time to correct the information. There are different reasons for inaccurate information, such as financial frauds, malicious rumors, and many other mistakes. Above all, the flow of information is an addiction to the financial markets, but uncertain information can create a lot of damage when you decide. As modern investors, if you rely on the headlines on financial sites and publications, you might overreact to the news and have to check for updates all the time to find reliable sources. Thus, it is better to focus on the market reaction before coming to any conclusion.

**The Right Resource**
If information streams in without a limit, the challenge of selecting the right resource can be daunting. The right resource and information are tied together. As a beginner, how will you find the

right resource amidst the crowd? Modern investors may feel lucky about having a myriad of choices and amazing free resources to gather details about investing. But too much of anything isn't always a good thing, right? As the saying goes, you will have to spend a lot of time researching if you want to find the right resources. I agree since there are so many facts about investing; for example, the way of calculating the ROI. However, there are situations where the investor gets confused about whether technical details mater over fundamentals. Over time, you will understand the ways to filter out the right information and make a proper decision. Until then, you might be overwhelmed with the options, suggestions, and overflowing information.

**Available Choices**

Don't you think too many choices create disturbance? Some might argue that it does not. But think about it. How will you feel when you have to research every choice before settling for a specific investment fund? For example, right now you are reading and learning about mutual fund because there are so many choices available. You don't want to fall into the trap of selecting an "oh-so-good" looking investment. The world of investment has so many choices, and that makes investors become tired even before selecting a single investment type. Sometimes, having a few options or choices is great, but if the investor is not vigilant, the best choice might be discounted. For example, someone who wants to make regular income will consider utility stocks because they pay dividends, yet he or she has better choices in mutual funds that will make things easier and simpler.

## Part of Advertising

Advertising is great, and it offers the chance to understand the investment vehicles in the industry. Even new investors can easily become familiar with investment vehicles in a short time. They'll be aware of most of the investments including bonds, index funds, mutual funds, and many others. In fact, they might be ready to explain the investment type to other investors without much effort. I accept that knowledge powered through advertising is great, but there are high chances for advertisements to push a new investor to select an investment that isn't worth their time and attention.

The best example I can share with you is mutual funds. So far, you've learned a lot about mutual funds. You know that it is one of the investments that require less work and attention. You are also aware that you have to pay a certain fee for professional management. An investor who completely relies on advertisements will not be aware of the fees because it won't be advertised. In this case, it is a problem for the investor who thought there are no fees involved with professional management. As a beginner, you must understand that advertisements will not always be something you can turn to.

Of course, there can be many investors who still stick to traditional methods while ignoring modern methods. Even though some investors like to stay with traditional methods, many modern investors feel safe when they have too much information. Having a wide range of information makes them feel confident when they make decisions. But if the information is streaming in, you'd have to be wise enough to settle for the reliable information. You just have to spend some time to evaluate what you see and gather. By evaluating, you'll be able to make wise decisions in investing.

Apart from these common problems, it is important to focus on the traps that investors regularly face. Before you invest, it is necessary to do some homework regarding your choice of investment because only then will you be able to stay away from the traps. You might select closed-end funds, bonds, stocks, or anything else. However, the important point is to be aware of the traps. Here are some traps related to mutual funds and how you can handle them successfully:

### You'll Come Across Fees That Can Be Avoided

There are certain fees related to mutual funds that can be avoided by the investor, but most beginners do not consider this or eventually fall into this trap. The 12b-1 fee is something that you can avoid, and it is no fun to handle these fees. The fee will be mentioned in the prospectus, and you can even find it on the funds' websites. However, there are mutual funds that do not charge a 12b-1 fee. If you find funds that charge you this fee, you have a selection of other funds that don't charge a 12b-1 fee. You don't have to worry or think that you would be left without choices because there are thousands of funds that you can choose from.

### You Don't Have To Bear Sales Charges

Most naïve investors worry about sales charges, and they believe it is a trap to get caught. Well, it is not! It will only be a trap if you consider it that way. Even though there are sale charges for certain mutual funds, you can still find no-load funds that do not include sales charges. So, if you have other options like no-load funds, why do you have to worry about sales charges?

## You Believe That It Lacks Liquidity

Before you believe everything you see on the internet, you must make sure to do some verification checkups. Of course, you might have come across the idea of less liquidity by reading blogs or books. But don't let such negative ideas overpower you. Before you conclude, think about mutual funds and other investment vehicles. Compare the level of liquidity and see whether a mutual fund has less liquidity? If you are selling a mutual fund, you can expect cash the next day. Thus, there shouldn't be a reason you believe that it lacks liquidity.

## An Assumption On Annual Capital Gains Distributions

If you have been tricked to believe that there are annual capital gains distributions for all mutual funds, it is time to clear the doubt. You must understand that there are no annual capital gain distributions for all mutual funds. For example, tax-efficient mutual funds and index mutual funds do not distribute each year. Also, these funds have lower-turnover, so it is not possible to make annual distributions. Even the retirement plans such as 401ks and IRAs are not subjected to capital gains distributions. However, there are different strategies that you can master in order to avoid capital gains distributions.

These are common traps that beginners get caught with. Most of the time, traps and investor's mindset correlates. If you consider the above traps, most of the traps are related to the way that investors think. Before you actually enter the investing industry, you tend to assume by reading blogs, books, and many other sources. It is not wrong to read and understand about the industry as much as possible. But you must know what you are reading. When you are selecting sources, make sure that they are reliable. Unreliable sources and information from unreliable sources can cause a lot of problems than you assume! Thus, it is better to double check before you decide anything and go straight into the investing industry!

# Chapter 7

# Detailed Information on the Mutual Fund Manager

Now that you are aware of the traps and the different types of mutual funds, it is time to learn about an important role played in mutual fund investing; the role of a mutual fund manager. Not only beginners, but even intermediary investors might not know about the role of a fund manager even though it is one of the essential roles played in the mutual fund investing industry. Some of you might ask why we should know the role of a fund manager. Well, you must know it because you'll be working with the manager hand in hand. In fact, they become your support pillar, so there are valid reasons why you must learn about fund managers and management. Let's begin.

The fund managers pursue the Chartered Financial Analyst (CFA) to begin their journey. The CFA candidates initially focus on portfolio management and investment analysis. The Chartered Financial Analyst work with researches regarding investments and investing recommendations. When these analysts work with fund management and operation, they understand their duties and responsibilities better. The ones who successfully complete their duties and responsibilities as CFAs tend to be promoted as managers whenever the opportunities come up.

There are so many responsibilities for a fund manager, but there are some specific everyday responsibilities that the manager has to handle. Basically, fund managers will research the best bonds, stocks, and other securities. Once they research, they determine the investment type that fits with the fund as per the prospectus. Sometimes, when there are large funds to handle, it will be difficult for the manager to do it alone. Thus, in such instances, the traders and support analysts will manage some of the activities. Some companies deal with multiple managers, so such companies make decisions through committee meetings. There are many other responsibilities of fund managers. Some of such responsibilities are focusing on fund performance, developing reports, finding out objectives and risks related to funds. You have a lot to learn about fund managers, so let's keep reading.

Even though I explained the role of a fund manager, it is important to understand how fund managers came into the picture. There's a particular index targeted by funds, so the main focus of a fund manager is beating the performance of a particular index. The "style-drift" is the way these fund managers follow. This deals with changing the target benchmark. The manager might underweight or overweight a few factors. Maybe the fund manager might reduce utilities or add any other factor against the benchmark index so that the returns increase. However, fund's prospectus includes the outline for the amount (minimum and maximum) a manager can wander off.

There are rating services that support the investors by focusing on categorized of funds and then, taking them into account for comparison. For example, Morningstar is one of the independent rating services, and top funds will earn 4/5 stars from its rating services. The expenses of these funds go above the target benchmarks. Just like this, the rating services will evaluate the fund's performance.

But remember, there are differences in index fund managers. The index fund managers work with a bit different purpose. As per the respective index, the fund manager will purchase all the stock, and this is called full-replication strategy. The manager must handle the fund's transactions and to trade stocks as per the relevant index. However, some funds may not buy ALL stocks, but rather some of the stocks. The concept is to adhere to the index's investment attributes. The manager will do their best to meet the underlying indexes requirements. A beginner will have some difficulties in understanding the market and how managers play their part. However, I have a lot more information regarding a fund manager's role.

You already know that the hardest part of investing can be managing portfolios if you didn't have the support of a fund manager. Initially, beginners fail to understand the importance of fund managers, but over time they understand the role played by the fund manager. A fund manager will handle funds actively or passively. Their management will create a huge difference in your portfolio, and you can't treat it as something simple. A fund manager's duty is considered pivotal because it can make or break your path.

When you invest in a mutual fund, you have to build portfolios, and it can be passive or active. Your fund manager will do the research, analysis, and the decision making whether to buy or sell funds or stocks. If your portfolio is actively managed, the manager will handle the components. Also, the fund manager's role will be decisive in regard to active mutual funds. If your portfolio is passive, the components will be handled by considering the underlying index. You must also have proper knowledge of the duties of mutual fund managers. Let's learn some of the duties in detail:

**Duty of Hiring**
It is not easy to handle all the responsibilities of the fund managers, so they seek help from professional firms and individuals. For example, duties such as getting capital, managing the brokers, and issuing reports are done by other professionals, basically, outsourced. They get the chance to hand over a few responsibilities to other professional firms that are capable of handling them. Yet, you must remember, even if they hand over their responsibilities to some other professionals, the fund managers are to be answered in regard to the funds' performance.

**Focusing on the Fund's Performance and Growth**
As mentioned above, another major duty of a fund manager is to focus on the fund's performance and growth. As per the investor's

objectives and expectations, the fund manager must decide on the way and place to invest. Even with the inflation rates and interest rates, the fund manager should be able to manage the performance of funds, and it becomes the basis to judge a fund managers performance.

**Handling the Wealth**

Investors and fund managers should have a good professional relationship. If both parties don't value the relationship, the investing journey will not be successful. The investor's wealth should be something that the fund manager values. He or she should protect and manage it successfully. This doesn't mean that the funds wouldn't go through risks because it will. Without risks, the fund manager will not be able to meet your investment goals. The point here is the fund manager must not handle your funds recklessly. Instead, they should be mindful about your funds. For example, if a decision is made to buy an asset(s), the fund manager should have done the research, and the decision should be made with due diligence. If the fund manager wants to handle the investor's wealth successfully, they must ensure to consider risk management techniques when evaluating a certain investment. This is just another way that fund managers can protect your wealth, but there are many other ways that a reputed fund manager might know of.

## Accordance with Regulatory Authorities

The fund managers should work in accordance with regulatory authorities and as beginners, you must be mindful about this factor. The rules set by the authorities should be respected and taken into consideration when managing your funds. The fund managers must be ready to meet the legislators when required because it ensures the reputation of the industry and the fund manager.

## Completing the Reporting Duties

This is one of the major duties of a fund manager. There are regulatory guidelines for reporting standards, so mutual fund managers should be aware of these details to avoid future issues. When building funds, the mutual fund manager must consider all the factors such as objectives, risks, strategies, and many other. Also, fund managers should check whether the investors work in accordance with rules and regulations. Last but not least, the fund manager must make sure to prepare documents on time while adhering to the rules and regulations.

Those are some of the main duties of a fund manager that every beginner must know of. Most beginners don't make an effort to learn the duties of a fund manager because they believe it doesn't concern them. If you know how important fund managers are for your investment journey, you will not avoid learning about them. However, the toughest part is selecting your fund manager. When you are selecting a fund manager, you must know that it is not a simple decision. They are the ones who play the main role in your journey, so even if it takes some time to make the right decision, it is okay. Usually, experienced investors focus on the fund management team and the manager. They focus on a few specific factors, so here's what you should know:

- Check whether the fund manager has successfully outperformed the benchmark.

- Check whether the fund manager focuses on other investors from different institutions.

- Check whether the fund manager has enough experience to help you with mutual fund investing.

- Check whether they identify market opportunities before their peers.

These are four basic points that you must consider when finding a fund manager. However, don't limit your search here because like I said, finding a fund manager is a huge decision. So, have you given a thought about the way managers make an investment decision? If you haven't, it can add great value on your journey. They already have the knowledge related to the subject, but their team is of great support for them. The research team gathers helpful insights. When they gather insights:

- They focus on volume of shifts in the market.

- They try to understand the macroeconomic outlook of the industry.

- They gather the desired (fund manager's desired companies) companies' annual results.

- They weight their information with the top managers before concluding anything.

Even though mutual fund investing is comparatively easy, there are risks associated with the industry. If you are planning to invest in mutual funds, you must have the support of a mutual fund manager and the knowledge to find the right fund. If you don't get these factors right, you'd have to face a lot of consequences. You must accept the fact that a mutual fund is a great choice to enhance your wealth. However, if you are looking for short-term benefits, you shouldn't consider this. Through perseverance and hard work, you'll find your path. Before moving to the next chapter, I have something interesting to share with you.

**Successful Fund Managers**

85-year old, Albert O. "Ab" Nicholas was one of the successful fund managers. He created the Nicholas Company, and he has handled the Morningstar rating services as well. Also, another noteworthy fund manager was Peter Lynch who directed the Fidelity Investments', Magellan Fund. From 1977 to 1990, he managed the equity portfolio of the company. Both of these successful fund managers are the ones who we can't stop talking about because they secured remarkable achievements in the investing industry.

When you are selecting a mutual fund manager, you must ensure to research, analyze, and then decide. I've repeatedly mentioned how important it is to select the right fund manager and the fund when you are investing in mutual funds. To build a great portfolio and to run a successful investing path, you must be ready to work hard. Through hard work, you can achieve anything that you want to, including becoming successful in mutual fund investing!

# Chapter 8

# What Are Your Investment Goals?

Having goals is an important part in everyone's life. More importantly, everyone has specific goals related to financing because it is one of the things that one must handle carefully. Before you invest, it is important to focus on personal goals and the way you set them. For example, are you planning for early retirement? Are you planning to build a house? Your goals can be anything that you want to achieve in life. So, what is an investment goal? Those are the goals that you want to achieve through your investment. Thus, when planning or setting your goals, you must spend time and think about the goals. For example, the money you save for retirement from your investments can be one of the investment goals. However, investment goals are personalized, so your goals don't have to be similar. You may have individual financial goals related to your investment. But sometimes, you may also have investment goals for your portfolio as well. For example, you might aim for an average return with time so that you can wait or a regular income.

Determining your investment goals can be tough if you don't understand how to create your own goals. You must talk to your financial advisor and understand the ways to set goals. Also, it is important to have a financial plan as well when you are dealing with investment goals. To prepare a financial plan, you must get advice from your financial advisor. There are three main factors that you must be aware of when you are setting the investment goals. These factors are risk tolerance, time horizon, and liquidity. Once you analyze these points you will be able to set specific goals as per your financial plan.

**Risk Tolerance**

Risk tolerance is one of the important factors to be considered. Are you ready to handle investment loses? Are you ready to accept when your investment fluctuates? Most beginners will not be ready to enter the investing industry if they know that there will be huge losses as much as they are huge profits. The ones who enter the market despite the risks are the ones who we call risk seekers. These investors are ready to take large losses because they know they will be able to make large profits as well.

But you can't determine where you stand that easily. Sometimes, you might feel as if you are a risk-seeker and other times you might feel as a risk-averse. If you don't determine this, it will be difficult to move on with investing. Thus, you must do an accurate assessment to decide where you stand. Most beginners think that they are risk-seekers, but the thought will change once they experience losses in investing. If the losses are painful, they might think twice before investing. So, you see, calling yourself a risk-seeker is not easy. Before you get into investing, you must check the situations when you will sell your investment. For example, will you sell your investment when you experience losses?

However, you must understand that investing will not work out unless you stick to your plan. You must have an understanding about the risk tolerance level if you want to build a successful plan and stick to it. Only then will you be able to achieve your investment goals.

**Time Horizon**
The important factor that deals with investment goal setting is time horizon. Basically, this is about the time period that you will allocate for the investment and it will directly impact your

investment goal. For example, are you investing to build a house in two years or to begin a business? Likewise, you must set goals with specific time frames. Even if you are dealing with mutual funds, you must select the right fund that meets your investment goal. Don't overlook the factor of time horizons because this is one of the crucial factors that you must adhere to.

**Liquidity**

Another important point that you must be aware of is liquidity. Your investment goals and liquidity have a close bond and investors consider liquidity as one of the important points. Basically, liquidity means the time taken to convert investment into cash. For example, if you are dealing with real estate, you can't liquidate it too soon. If you are investing in cash alternatives, you don't have to worry because they are highly liquidated. So, you must understand that the liquidity requirements that you have will impact your investment goals and your investment type. When you are dealing with liquidity, you should not only focus on the financial goal, but also the overall requirements.

These three factors will help you get a proper understanding about the investment goals and financial plan. Once you get these points clearly, you will be able to move on with the rest of the information related to investment goals. Think about how you will build a home without a proper plan. What will the results be? If you are super lucky, you'll end up building an amazing house. But we don't get lucky that often, right? So, probably you'll not get a satisfactory final outcome. The house might look like a disaster and you'll regret for spending so much in it.

Investing is just like this. Without investment goals and a plan, you might get lucky, but not all the time. If you don't have proper investment goals and a plan, you will not be able to meet your goals. However, there are different ways to meet your them. Typically, naïve investors' main concerns would be better returns without moving away from their comfort zones. But if you maintain goals when investing in different types of funds, you will be able to gain better returns as well as better exposure about the market. You must understand that if you set goals, you are likely to achieve them. In fact, you'll have the motivation to move forward in your investing journey. However, when you are setting goals, you must not forget the risks levels and the time horizon.

Whatever your target or goal is, you should not overlook your financial health. If you are vigilant, you should seek help and advice from professionals in the financial industry or you can easily get help from financial advisors. When you discuss with them, you'll be able to find investments that meets your preferred risks level. If you can't afford a financial advisor, you can become your own financial advisor. But for that, you must be ready to put in effort and time.

If you spend some time to understand the ways to set goals, you'll be able to run a successful investing career. Most of the time, investors forget the main concept of goal setting, which is setting up attainable goals. You must question yourself and ask why you are setting these goals. What are you planning to achieve from these goals? Have you written down your goals or do you just remember them? Don't you think writing down your goals will make things clearer and achievable? Also, if you write down your goals, you can show it to others and get some ideas. If you show it your friends or family, they might push you towards your goals. There are so many factors related to investment goals, so you can't consider it to be something simple. Also, don't forget to add value to your investment goals. There are many online calculators such as "College Savings Calculator" or "Retirement Calculator" to help you with this. Before you consider any of these calculators, make sure to do proper research. Once you set your investment objectives and goals, you will not find it hard to move on in your investing journey. However, I still have some tips to share with you. These tips will help you set successful investing goals. As I've mentioned before. a plan and a few investment goals are essential to lead a successful investing journey. Here are some of the tips that you must consider:

**Reason for Investing**

If you are investing, you must know the reason for it. If you are planning to invest in mutual fund investing, you must know why you have picked it. Maybe you liked mutual fund investing because it is easier than any other investments and you can make higher returns without spending a lot of time for the investment alone. However, you must know the reasons for your investments. Once you know the reason, you'll be able to set specific goals. These goals will help you stay motivated in investing.

## Realistic Ideas

Even though mutual fund investing is easy to get started, you will still need some time to gain returns from it. If you aim for quick returns, I don't think you will be able to become successful. Whatever you aim for should have realistic goals and ideas. Before you invest in any investment type, you must make sure to check the realities of the investment type. Once you understand the investment clearly, you will be able to set realistic goals. For example, don't think of investing $1000 per month when you don't have money for groceries. You should look at your situation and then decide!

## Break it Into Chunks

You should do this with not only investment goals, but with any life goals because they can be achieved if you break them into chunks. The chunks should be achievable. Most beginners frustrate themselves about not progressing enough. But when you frustrate yourself, you'll lose even more. So, don't frustrate yourself and begin small. When you start with a small, yet achievable monthly goal, you'll be able to achieve it. Once you achieve it, you'll be motivated to do more. When you look back at your smaller achievements, you will feel like it is possible to achieve bigger goals if you break them into chunks. Don't become greedy and start slow and move steadily. There is no point in starting with a huge sum of an amount if you are not going to move forward steadily. Thus, instead of creating unattainable goals and pushing yourself to achieve them, create smaller, attainable goals. Once you do this, you'll see yourself succeed and it will be a boost to do better.

**Begin with Simple Things**

If you start with the complex funds you are not going to be happy about it. There are mutual funds that are ideal for beginners and I'll be discussing them for you. Thus, when you are starting, don't try to begin with the investment type that pays a lot. Instead, start with the investment type that you know of. If there's a particular fund that you are well-versed with, you should go for it even if it is not as profitable as the complex ones. Right now, as a beginner, your focus should be in getting started with investing. If you just jump into the market and pick some random funds, you are going to regret it! While you invest in something simple, spend time and research about other investments as well. Once you become successful with simple investments, you can slowly move on to the more complex ones. However, even if you are investing in something simple, you must try to understand the way it works. When you get to enjoy regular success, you will get the interest to look for more opportunities. Thus, establish small and grow bigger!

Setting up goals or understanding what your investment goals are is not easy. Of course, it will take some time. You might have to read a lot and research more. But you have no excuse when it comes to setting up goals. If you set goals, you will see the investment path clearly!

## Chapter 9

## How to Manage Your Investment?

We've discussed investment goals, so now, let's learn the investment strategies. If you have defined goals and you are aware of the money required, then you have to focus on the investment strategy. What actually is an investment strategy? It is more like a guide that focuses on your risk tolerance, goals, and many other factors. There are two main factors that you need to know about when settling for an investment strategy and they are:

**Begin Right Now**
Beginners often put off things for another time when they are new to investing. But with an investment strategy, you can't do it. You should not put off your goals for another time because investment strategies are one of the essential factors of investing and it will help you get started. Not having a proper investment strategy can impact your investment journey.

## Focus on Diversification

The strategy of diversification is important than anything else. You can meet your goals through diversification because you'll be investing in different investments, so the risks are not limited to one investment. If you invest all your money in one investment type, you'd be completely washed out if the market falls. It is better to invest in different asset classes. If you do so, you will be able to cover a few parts of the market.

Nothing is as great as information. If you know more about investments and investment options, you'll be able to make a better decision. In fact, when you have more information, you will be able to make more informed decisions. You will also get the chance to create successful investment strategies. Let's think about mutual fund investment strategies. What do you know about them? There are no special rules for mutual fund investment strategies, but there are different strategies for mutual fund investment. However, just like other investments strategies, you must make sure to understand the objectives and the market conditions as well. If you don't get these factors right, it will be difficult to come up with the right strategies. As I've said before, there are different strategies for mutual fund investing. Certain strategies are limited to the ability mangers have at managing money, regulatory issues, sponsors desire, and as per the investors demand. Before you learn the investment strategies, try to understand the outline for investment strategies.

## Mutual Fund Categorization

The type of assets and policy statements are the factors that help to classify mutual funds. The categorization of the mutual fund is helpful when creating investment strategies. There are broad categories in mutual funds, for example, equity funds that hold equities or common stocks. Fixed income funds can be another example because it holds fixed income securities. However, there are different categories of funds available in mutual funds. When you are developing investment strategies, you must make sure to consider this factor.

## Name of the Fund

Public prospectus' and trust indentures will include the investment policies of the funds, and those policies will have an impact on the investment strategies. The managers focus on the fund's assets when this happens, and it has made a few funds to lose the power to resemble its name. Some of the funds that perform differently than the way its name suggests have gained concerns from the regulators. For example, In Canada, the Mortgage and Income Fund held a lot of equities and very few mortgages or bonds. Even though the fund was performing well, it was classified to the Income Fund section in many surveys. But professionals stated that this fund should be classified under the Balanced or Equity Fund.

There are many factors that you must take into consideration when developing investment strategies. The mutual fund strategies have a great impact on the organization and the types of funds invested in.

Even though many beginners might not understand the importance of categorization, it is one of the important factors when marketing mutual funds. When categorization of funds is not clear, there can be a lot of problems, which includes the difficulties in creating the right investment strategy. Once you build your mutual fund portfolio, you must do the needful to maintain it. If you don't maintain it, you will not be able to achieve your investment goals. With that being said, let's take a look at four main strategies that will help you manage your portfolio.

**Market-Timing Strategy**

This strategy deals with getting to the markets, assets, and sectors at a given time. Timing the market is an excellent opportunity for the investors, and if that happens, the investor will be able to sell high and buy low. However, some of the investors use this strategy too often, and it is not healthy. If you let your emotions get in the way, you will not be able to make logical decisions. In investing, it is essential to make decisions logically than emotionally. Many investors don't believe in market timing, and they think that marketing-timing strategy doesn't work. Of course, it is not possible to predict the future, but there are market-timing indicators that you can use.

**Wing-It Strategy**

This is one of the common strategies that you will see in the mutual fund industry once you become familiar with it. If your mutual fund portfolio has no structure or plan, then you are using the wing-it strategy. If you want to develop your portfolio, you'd want to add more money. So, when you are deciding , how will you know which fund, stock, or asset you should invest in? Are you planning to find new investments? If you don't have a plan and if you are utilizing the wing-it strategy, you are going to face difficulties. Many professionals agree that this is a successful strategy. Thus, you must have a structure or a plan to make things easier. I have included this strategy to the list not because it is going to help you build your portfolio, but only so you know what to avoid if you want to develop your portfolio.

**Buy-and-Hold Strategy**

This is another interesting strategy that you can consider. Usually, you'll have a higher chance of profiting when you use this strategy. When you utilize this strategy, you will think that this is easier than any other strategy. But it doesn't mean that you are going to make profits alone; you will face losses as well. The buy-and-hold technique is much better when compared to other strategies.

**Performance-Weighting Strategy**

This is something that adds both the buy-and-hold and timing strategy together. If you use this strategy, you might check your portfolio often to make adjustments if required. For example, let's say in 2016 you started with $100,000 in equity with four funds in your portfolio and these funds spilled into 25% weightings each. After 2016, you will see that the weighting is not equal between the four funds because some funds would have performed well.

Performance weighting is when you sell the best funds and buy the worst funds. But when you think about this, you will not feel great about this logic, and you might want to go against this. Don't let your emotions decide what you should and not do. Focus on the theory and the strategy and work accordingly. If you want to benefit from this strategy, you must be a disciplined individual.

You must not use a strategy just because you "feel" like or someone recommended. Instead, you must use a strategy after you've done your homework. You already know the importance of having a strategy, so don't take it lightly. Now let's discuss a few tips that might be helpful for beginners when investing in a mutual fund.

It is true that mutual funds have become one of the best investment options for people who want to enhance their savings. The flexibility of mutual funds has become one of the reasons why they are popular. Even though mutual funds have so many benefits, some risks make individuals aware of what to consider. Many beginners don't pay attention to risks, and they believe all mutual funds are pretty straightforward and similar. Like I've already explained, there are subcategories for mutual funds such as debt, equity, and hybrid funds. These funds differ due to different factors such as thematic exposure, investment horizon, asset classes, and tax treatment. It is evident that beginners might get overwhelmed when they witness these choices. However, here's a few tips, so you can get the best returns from your investment as a beginner:

*Keep objectives clear*: to keep your objectives clear, you must consider two main points, which is the amount and the time duration. You must know how much you are going to invest and how long you are going to remain in the market. Of course, mutual funds are one of the financially flexible products. Even if you have a small amount, you can get started with that amount. Also, if you want to redeem or invest in mutual funds whenever you want, there are a few exceptions, of course. This offers you the chance to select the investment type that you need by not forgetting your objective. For example, if you want to invest in a mutual fund with a short-term trading motive, then you can consider a debt fund or liquid fund as they have high liquidity and minimum risks. However, there are different options that you can consider when you are dealing with mutual fund investing.

*Be updated about the risks.* Risks are not minor factors to ignore and they have the power to break or make your investment. So, you must make sure you focus on the risks related to the investment opportunities. Every fund in mutual funds involves some level of risks. You must not forget that equity funds such as small-cap and mid funds have higher risks, but they have the ability to offer better rewards. On the other hand, if you look for low risks and lower returns because you don't want to handle risks, then you must consider debt funds. You must spend time to understand the risk-return formula of each fund. If you understand the formula, you will be able to select the fund as per your interest regarding risks.

*Diversify the investments.* Through mutual funds, you will be able to diversify investments. For example, if you are in a bullish market and if you want to grow your investment, you can consider investing in a small cap or mid-cap fund that would offer a higher return. Similarly, there are debt funds for short-term that have lower risks so you can consider them if you want low-risk options. There are many other ways to diversify your investment that have the power to balance the risk and return of your portfolio.

*Periodic monitoring.* Your success should be monitored periodically. Often, investors ignore considering their mutual funds' investment performance. It is essential to examine the funds' performance because it helps you understand whether you are on the right track or not. When the investors monitor their performance, they will be able to find out the investment that works verses the ones that don't. If the investor has the information regarding the performance, he or she will be able to make decisions regarding the poorly performing funds. Also, periodic monitoring is helpful to enhance the long-term growth of your portfolio.

*NAV's role.* Of course, NAV doesn't decide how funds performs or how it will perform. This is the reason why returns from mutual funds are calculated by percentage. Even if you have purchased funds with low or high NAV, your investment growth will be in percentage as per the funds' performance.

If you are not aware of these tips, you are likely to make silly mistakes that will lead to huge losses. However, if you are looking for "quick rich" methods, you must focus on long-term investments to get higher returns. If your investment horizon is above five years, you can consider mutual funds that are equity oriented. Equity markets are volatile, but as for the historical data, the equity markets have moved in a positive direction, so it is beneficial to the investors. However, investing in mutual funds is not a decision that you directly make. Instead, you have to do a lot of research and understand because the decision should be perfect!

## Chapter 10

## What Are Your Investment Strategies?

We have learned about the investment goals and strategies about managing your investment. However, there is a lot more to learn about managing your investment. There are factors such as where to buy, investment fees, passive or active management, and creating a plan that comes together when focusing on the ways to manage your investment. When you are managing your investment or making financial decisions, you must be confident. Mutual funds are one of the major investment types in the investing world. The aim of the mutual fund is clear, which is to diversify risks at a lower rate. However, there are five main factors that you must consider when buying mutual funds. Here we go:

**1. Think about active or passive management**
Before you do anything, you must think about whether you want to mimic the market or beat it. You can decide it based on the costs and results. If you are into active management, you must

understand that professionals handle actively managed funds. They research everything about the market and the fund, and they buy funds with the intention to beat the market. There are a few fund managers who were able to make this happen in the short run. It has become tough to gain benefits overtime because funds are expensive due to human involvement. On the other hand, passive investing is becoming popular. Most people prefer this because it is cheaper and involves lower fees. The index fund is one of the best passive investment. When an investor invests in a few index funds securities, it will represent the whole market.

For example, the S&P 500 fund holding mirrors the 500 stocks in index funds. The performance of the fund will replicate the index fund itself. Hence, if the news mentions a 3% increment for the S&P 500 for a day, it will benefit your index fund as well. Also, you don't have to bear any management fees as there will not be any real management. Basically, passive management is cheaper than active management.

However, don't stop looking for more information until you feel comfortable with a specific management.

## 2. Budget calculation

When you think about budgeting, you must remember it is essential to be patient. A simple fact is you must agree and feel comfortable about the money you leave in the market for a few years even if there are downturns in the market. There are different ways to budget but let me provide you with some ideas.

You must know the amount that you need to invest in a mutual fund. Often, you'd be required to pay a minimum amount by the mutual fund providers if you want to open an account. There are some brokers with no minimum amount rules, but some others have different amounts. Thus, you have to inquire about it from a broker.

Once you have decided the amount, you have to think about a way to invest it. As you've already learned, mutual funds are great due to its low-cost scheme. You can diversify your mutual fund portfolio by investing in stocks, and it will help the growth of your portfolio. Also, you can invest in bonds to gain steady returns even though it will take some time. So typically, younger investors will be ready to take risks to get better returns. But the investors who are close to their retirement age will be interested in having more holdings. However, there are different ways that you can consider when you are budgeting.

## 3. The place to purchase mutual funds

If you are investing in stocks, you must have a brokerage account. But if you are investing in mutual funds, there are different choices. There are retirement accounts that make you invest in mutual funds eventually, for example, if you have contributed to 401(k), then it is highly possible that you have invested already. There are fund companies such as BlackRock Funds and Vanguard, so you can purchase from these companies. When you are purchasing from these companies, you will have a few choices to pick from.

Many investors prefer online brokerages because they can access a wide range of funds from different companies. But when you are dealing with a broker, there are a few factors that you must consider:

*Fund choices.* Even though retirement plans offer a wide range of mutual funds, you might look for more choices than that. If you are looking for more choices, the best way is to connect with a broker. A broker offers thousands of choices with the no-transaction-fee. You can also consider other types such as ETFs. ETFs offer the benefit of diversification but must be traded like stocks. However, if you are dealing with a broker, you have the chance to select funds among the pool of choices.

*Easy to handle.* You must ensure that the brokerage's app or website is easy to handle. If it is not, then there is no point in obtaining such services.

*Research tools.* Don't pick a random broker; take time to think and research. The broker you work with must help you in learning about the funds. He orshe must ensure that you are ready to invest your money.

*Affordability.* You would have to bear the transaction fees charged by the brokerage account so be mindful about it.

### 4. Understanding the fees and charges.

You already know that active management will be costly, so you have to bear higher fees. Despite the management type, you'd have to bear an annual fee because the fund management company will charge a certain amount. You'd have to deal with an expense ratio as well as the costs related to running the fund. For example, if it is a 1% expense ratio, you'd have to pay $10 for $1000 each time you invest. Even though you can't understand all the fees upfront, it is better if you can spend some time to understand as much as possible because they have the power to eat your returns.

You might not deal with commissions when investing in mutual funds, but you'd have to manage transaction fees. We've already discussed load funds, which is when you pay a certain amount to the broker who acts like commission, but it is sold by sales. But you have a great chance in regard to fees where you can consider no-transaction fees funds that are offered by the broker.

## 5. Create and manage the portfolio

This is an essential point that you must be aware of. Once you have decided the fund type and the ways to invest and everything, it is time to manage the investment.

A simple tip is to revisit your portfolio every year and check whether it still matches your diversification goal. We have discussed a strategy that you can incorporate when you are revisiting your portfolio. You must ensure that your portfolio has the balance that it should have.

Another important tip is to stick to the plan. Before you started investing, you might have had a plan, so don't divert your eyes from the plan. A plan helps to chase the performance. However, you should read a fund and check how it performed last year. Most fund investors do check and read the performance before making a decision. The point here is there are certain investing goals that you should set and if you don't stick to the goals, you are unlikely to reach your final target.

If you understand these five main factors, you will be able to get started with mutual fund investing in an easy way. So now, let's understand the ways to manage investment risks successfully.

## *Ways to manage investment risk*

Mutual funds deal with risks whether its debt, equity or any other investments. There are different levels of risks for different types of funds. There different schemes and requirements for mutual funds, so when you are investing , you'd have to consider all these factors. All of these factors impacts the risks level of investment. The best part about mutual fund investing is that you get to reduce the risks of investment using different strategies. Here are a few ways you can utilize to reduce the risk of your portfolio:

## *Invest in diversified equity schemes*

Most beginners make the mistake of investing in funds by checking the previous year's performance of the funds. These choices often offer positive returns in consideration to a particular sector of the market. So, when investors invest in such funds, they are getting themselves into the riskier investments. Rather than investing in these funds that have great exposure to a certain sector, you can consider investing in diversified equity schemes. This would reduce the risk and volatility related to your portfolio.

### *Risk tolerance level*

Without struggling to time the market, you can spend your time to understand the role of emotions that are being played in relations to the risks level. One of the key factors that you need in order to achieve success in the mutual fund is handling risks and knowing the risk level that you are comfortable with. When the investors have a clear view on this, they will be able to focus on their performances and investment goals. There are different types of people who deal with risks in different ways. Now, let's have a look at some of them to understand more about emotions and risks tolerance:

*Managers.* These investors are overconfident, and they treat themselves as experts. Their overconfidence blindsides the apparent risks.

*Avoiders.* These investors often avoid losses. They don't prefer taking up risk, and they listen to the inner voice that stops them from reaching their goals. These investors settle for lower returns because they avoid risks. But remember, the long-term growth will be questionable if investors settle for lower returns.

*Seekers.* Some investors love taking higher risks even though they are not comfortable with that level. They are thrill seekers, so they look for risks and this is not healthy!

*Researchers.* These investors are the ones who take risks, but not without proper research. They make sure to do research regarding the risk rate before deciding to invest in a particular investment type. Also, these investors tend to be nervous because they fear market fluctuations.

However, you can't actually say that you fit into this or that group of investors because you have just started your journey. Your way of investing has a lot to do with your portfolio's growth. If you are aware of what you are doing, you will be able to manage your investment portfolio while taking a comfortable rate of risks.

### *Two main risk indicators*

Even though five indicators deal with the risks of investment, I'm going to share two main indicators with you. As a beginner, you might find these indicators beneficial. Alpha and Beta are the main risk indicators that we are about to discuss. The modern portfolio theory (MPT) major components are these indicators. However, MPT is an academic methodology that is utilized to find the performance of mutual fund investments in comparison to market benchmarks. These risk indicators help the investors to find the risk-reward framework of the investments. Let's briefly learn about the indicators.

*Alpha*

This is used in order to calculate the performance of an investment on the basis of risk-adjustment. The volatility of the fund portfolio and the risk-adjusted performance are compared to the benchmark index. The relative investment's excess return to the benchmark index's return is its alpha. Basically, the returns from the portfolio funds subtracted or added to the portfolio manager's value is represented as the alpha. The performance fund's benchmark index is decided by alpha. If alpha is 1.0, it indicates outperformance and if alpha is -1.0, it indicates under-performance. For investors, the alpha should be higher to benefit from the investment.

*Beta*

This is about coefficient measurements. This measures the security's symmetric risk or volatility, or the portfolio is compared to the whole market. The regression analysis helps the investors to find the response of investment's return to the market movements. As for definition, 1.0 is the market beta. So, the portfolio values will be measured on how they move away from the market.

The 1.0 beta means investment's price will move closely with the market. Anything less than 1.0 means you must handle fewer volatile investments when compared to the market. Similarly, the 1.0 beta or if the beta is more than that indicates high volatility compared to the market.

If you are one of the conservative investors, you must focus on fund portfolios and securities that have low betas. If you are willing to handle more risks, you must consider investments with high betas. However, alpha and beta are just two of the indicators, but there are three more that you must learn about. Even though these two indicators are incredibly important for beginners, it is better if you can invest your time in learning other indicators as well.

You should understand that if you want to manage your investment and your investment portfolio, you must know all five of these indicators as well. Also, don't forget the fact that mutual fund returns are linked with market conditions. Thus, you must not dream of huge returns in a short-term because it is not possible. Like we discussed earlier, you must have realistic expectations if you want to achieve your investment goals. Remember, you must have the self-discipline to remain in the market!

## Chapter 11

# Selecting and Utilizing the Mutual Fund

The most crucial part of investing is selecting and utilizing the mutual fund. Most beginners struggle with regards to this, and that's the reason why I want to discuss this particular topic with you. So, how will you pick the ideal mutual fund that suits your investment goals? Are you planning to invest in a mutual fund, but you are confused about selecting the right fund? Most beginners have the same issue when selecting the right mutual fund. Even though you think that selecting a mutual fund is a big deal, it is certainly not if you understand the way it works. Let's understand the ways to select the right mutual fund to invest in.

Before you select a mutual fund, you must understand your goals. If you don't have clear goals, you will not be able to utilize your money in the right way. Are you focusing on long-term gains or are you focusing on your current income? What are you hoping to do with the money that you get from investing? Even though there is a wide range of selections available in the market, you have to make sure that your goals are clear.

Along with goals, you must also focus on the level of risks. Are you ready to handle the value swings in your portfolio or are you a person with conservative investment? Of course, if you don't have the ability to handle risks, then entering the mutual fund investing industry is questionable. With that be said, let's look at a few points that you must consider when selecting a suitable mutual fund:

**Focus on The Fund Type and The Style**

The growth funds are for capital appreciation. If your focus is on a long-term plan, you can consider growth funds. But you must be ready to handle volatility and risks. These funds include common stocks. Thus, it is volatile. Even though they are highly risky, you'll be able to gain better returns with time. If you are considering these funds, you must accept the time frame as well, which is mostly 5-10 years.

Basically, capital appreciation funds will not pay dividends. For someone who's looking for current income, this may not be the right choice. Instead, he or she can consider income funds. These funds include debt instruments and bonds as they pay regular interest. Like we already discussed, corporate debt and government bonds are common in income funds. The bond funds will have different time horizons, so you must be considerate about it as well. Certain bond funds have less volatility and negative or low correlation in regard to the stock market. Therefore, you can consider them as a great choice for diversification in your stock portfolio. You must not forget the fact that bond funds are risky even though they are less volatile. Most investors consider bond funds because they can diversify their portfolio even though they are risky.

Of course, as a beginner, you must do your research before you settle for a specific fund because you don't want to fall into the traps. There are many other great alternatives available in a mutual fund, but what matters is when you are selecting the fund, you must make sure to check whether it matches your investment goals.

**Check The Fees and Charges**
Beginners often overlook fees and charges because they just want to get started. They don't want to think about the charges and fees, but only when they have to pay or bear the costs, they tend to think about it. But remember, if you begin your journey without proper understanding you might have to face a lot of problems eventually.

There are different types of charges and fees associated with investing. Thus, before you invest, you must get a clear idea about it. We've discussed sales charges, an example being load. This will be charged when selling an investment or when purchasing. The amount paid from the initial investment when you buy shares is a front-end load fee, and you'd have to bear it. The back-end load fee is required when you sell shares that are in the fund.

Even though charge front-end and back-end loads can be 8.5% by law, normally investors are charged 3%-6% from the amount distributed or invested. The aim of charging these fees is to prevent turnover and to collect the administrative charges of investment. As per the type of the fund, the payment may reach the fund itself or the broker. The level-load fee is charged from the assets that are in the fund, and it's an annual charge. You are aware that no-load funds deal with management expense ratio and other charges, except for front and back-end fee. However, other charges of the no-load fund can be high.

The 12b-1 fees apply to other funds, and they are included in the share price. During the distribution of shares in the fund, the fees may be used for promotions and other activities. Most of the time, the investor will not be aware of this fee. However, by law, the 12b-1 fee is 0.75% of the average annual assets in the fund.

As a beginner, you must not forget to learn management ratio because it helps you understand charges and fees. The ratio explains the percentage of assets in the fund that is in order to meet the fund expenses. If your ratio is higher, your return will be lower and vice-versa.

## Get Clear About Past Results and Portfolio Managers

You must understand that portfolio managers are one of the essential roles in your investment journey. You can't ignore them. Just like that, you can't ignore the past results of the funds. Before you invest, you must make sure to research the past results of the funds. When you are reviewing the past results and portfolio managers, you must consider the following points:

- Check whether the fund manager has provided results that meet the market returns.

- Check whether the fund has gained returns dramatically in a year. The focus should be on the volatility of the fund and the major indexes.

- Check whether the turnover is unusually high. If yes, the tax liabilities will be larger.

If you evaluate these points, you will be able to understand the performance of the fund managers in different situations, and you can have a proper idea of the past results of the fund. Before you invest in a particular fund, it is better to talk to the investment manager. You will get some idea about the prospectus, market trends, and many other factors that impact the performance of the funds.

**Think About The Things That Matter**

Most beginners think about history whenever they want to make a decision about mutual funds. Don't you think it is better to focus on the factors that will impact the future results of the fund? Let me share an example with you in this case. I mentioned about Morningstar, Inc., and this is one of the famous research firms in the investment industry. Even though they have been using star rating as per the risk-return adjustments of the funds, they have later found out that the correlation between future success and the ratings is low. Thus, they understood that there is no point in focusing on the things that mattered less, rather they introduced a different system to grade the funds. The new system is the five P's system. The five P's People, Price, Parent, Process, and Performance. By using this new system, the company focuses on the fund's expense ratio, investment strategy, manager's longevity, and many other factors. Based on the category, the funds will receive a relevant rating.

This example above teaches you that there is no point in relying on history if it doesn't provide help to make future decisions. You must think about the things that really matter and provide value to your decision.

The main factor that correlates with the performance of the fund is its fees. You will be able to understand the validation of this statement if you think about ETF. Anyway, I understand that as a beginner you are tempted to focus on the changes that happens in the past. But if you want to select the right fund, you must focus on the factors that impact future success.

We've discussed a few factors that helps to select the right mutual fund. However, you must have an interest in knowing when you enter into a new industry. If you aim to make money without working for it, I don't think you'll get to earn legally. Even though mutual fund investing doesn't require a lot of time and hard work, you still need to spend time learning it!

## Avoid These Mistakes When Selecting Mutual Funds

If you are vigilant, you'll be able to benefit from mutual funds without losing big money. Most beginners are not careful when they are starting their journey, so it leads them towards huge losses. You might think that funds advertised in the media are great and won't hurt to try. While it won't hurt to try, it will definitely break you. Even though we have discussed selecting the right mutual funds, it is essential to focus on the mistakes that you must avoid when selecting mutual funds. Often, beginners avoid learning these mistakes, but it is not a wise move. If you make these mistakes, you might end up facing exorbitant fees or even lose your interest to invest in mutual funds. With that being said, let's look at a few common mistakes made by investors when selecting mutual funds:

## Researching On Past Performances

We've already discussed the importance of considering the factors that impact the future success of a fund. Yet, most investors waste their time researching the past performance because they believe they'll get the same returns. You must understand that the past performance of a fund doesn't decide the future performance. Besides, even if a fund worked well for the past five years, it doesn't mean that it will continue that way. As a beginner, you must consider the time horizon, risk tolerance, and many other factors that will help you understand a fund's performance. Of course, past performances of a fund might provide some clarity or idea, but you shouldn't consider it as the basis for selecting the right fund.

## Not Focusing On Tax Implications

Many investors use retirement accounts to benefit from mutual funds, but they might also invest outside of their account that may lead to tax events. There are different reasons for tax events, and one of those reasons is actively managed funds that has higher turnover. Typically, mutual funds that have higher returns tend to face tax events, thus, as beginners you have to be aware of it.

## Overpaying Fees

Apparently, when you are dealing with mutual funds you would have to handle different fees. The fees and percentage of fees will differ as per the fund that you select. The actively managed funds will deal with higher fees when compared to funds that are passively managed. There are many other fees apart from management fees. For example, some mutual funds deal with brokers so for them, it is important to pay commissions (front-end load). If you don't want to overpay fees, you can consider a no-load fund as it is not associated with commission. So, if you don't focus on the fees, you'd end up losing all your returns.

## Not Being Considerate About Overlapping Investments

You shouldn't think that you can invest in a mutual fund and forget about it entirely even without focusing on the underlying investment that is in the fund. Most investors make this mistake, but you shouldn't if you own more than one fund. When you diversify your investments, you must make sure to do the necessary requirements. Perhaps, nobody wants to hold similar investments in different funds. The main idea of the mutual fund is to diversify in industries and classes. So, if you are holding the same bond or stock in your fund, it doesn't justify the idea of diversification. If you don't spread out the investment, you'll fall badly when the market tanks. You must be mindful about this mistake as well.

Nevertheless, you must accept that mutual funds are an excellent choice for investors to create wealth, but you should not look for a risk-free option because there isn't any, including mutual funds. If you don't want to face higher risks, you must know to control the risks by paying attention to the required areas. You can select and utilize the best mutual fund, but you must not forget to consider the mistakes that you might make. Once you have a clear understanding, you can invest freely!

## Chapter 12

## Ways To Analyze Your Fund Performance

If you think you just have to invest and that's it, you are wrong! You have to stay on the lookout for what's happening. You have to focus on the performance of mutual funds to decide whether it is working as you wanted it to. So, you must analyze the fund's performance. How will you do it? Like I already mentioned, past performances will not decide your future results. However, knowing the past performances will not hurt either. Although, you must know to analyze the fund while focusing on the factors to avoid. Once you get these things clear, you will be able to make informed decisions that will help you meet your expectations in investing.

**Appropriate Benchmarks And Funds**

The very first method to analyze a mutual fund's performance is by comparing the returns from the fund to a suitable benchmark. If you want to check the performance of your fund, you must compare the fund to its average return of a similar category. For example, assume that you've got a 401(k) statement that states a large decline of one of the funds while others have not declined in a certain time period. This doesn't mean you should remove the declining fund from your portfolio. Before you conclude, make sure to focus on the fund categories and types and check whether they have a similar performance. Also, for a benchmark, you can consider an index fund as well. It is important to have a broader perspective about the benchmark and the funds as they have a direct influence on the fund's performance.

## Differentiate Good Performance That Might Turn Otherwise

Say you are investing in a stock fund; you'll have a plan for three or more years. With this assumption, you don't have to think about the time frame that is less than 3 years. This doesn't mean that short-term returns are peripheral. Yes, sometimes a good performance can be a negative factor too. There are a few reasons why good performance in a year can be a negative factor. If there are unusual returns in a year, it can be abnormal. Also, investing shouldn't be something exciting that you make quick returns from the start of your journey. Instead, it should be something that you do with extreme focus and attention. I can add another reason as well, which is a higher short-term performance of a fund might attract even more assets.

If you have a smaller amount, it is possible to manage and even during the market shifts you'd be able to handle the money. Also, you can't expect a fund that performed well this year to do the same next year. It doesn't happen that way because many factors affect the fund's performance. In fact, if assets in your fund increases, it can be challenging for the prospects of the fund as well as for the future performance. If you select the right fund manager, he or she will handle your portfolio accordingly.

**Focus On The Economic Cycles**
If you seek advice from a few investment advisors, you'll receive different advices regarding the time period to analyze the performance of the funds. Most of the advice will be regarding short-term performance, which can be a year or less and it will not provide enough information about the future of the fund performance. There are instances where even best fund managers have faced a bad year.

The managers calculate the actively-managed funds' risks to outperform the benchmark. So, the poor performance within a year will indicate that the manager has not met expected results. However, without understanding the economic cycles, you will not be able to have a clear understanding of the performance of the funds. As beginners, your duty is to educate yourself about economic cycles and market movements.

**Find The Manager Tenure**
The manager tenure is for actively managed funds. The term refers to the time allocated by the management team for handling a certain fund. The time is often calculated in years. If you are investing in actively managed funds, it is mandatory to know about manager

tenure. The managers who manage actively managed funds try to outperform the benchmark, for example, the S&P 500. On the other hand, the passively managed funds will not be treated that way. Instead, the manager will focus only on investing in similar securities.

If you want to get a clear idea about your fund, it is essential to know about the manager tenure for the fund that you are planning to consider. For example, if your interest is for a mutual fund that has a 3-year return, but the tenure is or a year. Then, there's a clash between management and your expectations, so you have to reconsider this decision. So, for this, you must ensure to research before you consider a particular fund.

**Know About Expense Ratio**

When you think about funds, you must understand that they don't manage themselves. Since they don't run by themselves, management comes into the picture, and that's why you have to learn about fees related to it. If you assume that higher expense means higher returns, you're wrong because and it doesn't work that way. Mostly, lower expenses provide higher returns when you operate with a long term basis. But, how will you decide the expense ratio to consider mutual fund performance? You must know the average ratios of the funds, so here are some of the examples:

- Foreign Stock Funds: 1.50%

- S&P 500 Index Funds: 0.15%

- Bond Funds: 0.90%

- Large-Cap Stock Funds-1.25%

You must ensure not to buy funds that have high expense ratios. Know that average expenses differ as per the fund category. The research costs regarding portfolio management will be higher for areas where there isn't enough information. For example, information about domestic companies can be easily gathered compared to other niches.

### Think About The 5 And 10-Year Periods Of Performance

Even though fund managers tend to face a bad year once in a while, there are fund managers who do better due to particular economic environments. Thus, they extend the time frames. An example would be if a fund manager works with the conservative philosophy about getting higher performance in poor economic conditions and vise-versa. The performance of the fund may not look strong now, but if you think about the 2-3 year time period, how would it be?

The fund management style sometimes accepts market conditions and sometimes it does not. Thus, it is vigilant to focus on the skills of a fund manager when considering the performance of a fund over a period of time.

Actually, if you look at the economic cycles, a complete cycle will grow and recessionary periods as well in 5-7 years. During this time, the economy might face a recession for a year. Similarly, there can be 4-5 years of growth during this time. So, when you are analyzing funds and you find a fund that has higher returns in five years, you can explore more about it. However, as a beginner, you should never make decisions without researching more about the fund and its performance.

Also, it is better to utilize the weights to measure method to analyze the performance of the funds. You can consider mutual fund research sites to check fund performances using this method. The weighting method helps you to select the funds by analyzing the performance along with ideas about future performances. I'll mention a few research sites that you can consider to meet your needs.

### Research Sites For Mutual Funds

The internet is useful if you use it wisely. Some beginners look for information from all the sites that they see. But you should be aware. Not all sites are reliable like you may assume. When you are using different sites to research or to find information, you must make sure that they are reliable. Collecting unreliable information will not help you make proper decisions in investing. However, there are tools online that will help you compare and analyze the funds with a few steps. Even if you are not utilizing this method, you can still consider these sites to study mutual funds or to find new details about mutual funds. You must know that every site differs from one another and their services differ too, hence before using it you must sample the sites. If you trail the sites, you will be able to find whether they fit your needs or not. Here we go:

**Morningstar:** We've already learned about this system, so you know that this is a star rating system. The ratings will be on a scale of 1-5, however, now they are developing a new system. The rating system helps investors find the right mutual funds that meet the expectations of the investors.

Along with the rating system, there are many other services and tools offered by Morningstar. The tools are researching facility for all levels of mutual funds, software for experts, and so much more. The commentary and information from Morningstar are extended to hedge funds and mutual funds as well. If you are a beginner, you can opt for the free option, or if you are willing to pay, you can consider the premium version.

**FundReveal:** If you are interested in actively managed funds and if you want to gather the information you must consider this site. You'll be able to evaluate the performance of a fund with the help of this tool. It is also important to know that the results obtained from this site will not be upon subjective analysis, past total returns, opinions, popularity contests or hunches. This is not a site associated with brokerage firms, investment firms or any companies, so you can accept their unbiased services. As I mentioned, they don't focus on the past total returns. Instead, they consider the daily average returns. If the funds are analyzed this way, the investor gets more knowledge regarding future predictions of the funds.

**Lipper leaders:** Lipper is considered a global leader that provides information, commentary, and analytical tools related to mutual funds. This research tool is handy for individual investors, fund advisors, and other related professionals. They stick to their five metrics named "Leaders," and it consists of consistent return, total return, expense, tax efficiency, and preservation.

**MAXfunds:** This site offers a tool named "Fund-O-Matic Fund Screener," so by using this tool the best fund can be found. You don't need a finance degree to find the right mutual fund, and instead, you can use this site. This is for regular people, so you will find it easy to browse as well. You can find quality, yet less costly funds to invest in.

**Kiplinger mutual fund finder:** You can use this comparison tool provided by a trusted financial resource. The investors get the opportunity to research a fund. You can even find a fund that matches certain criteria. There are many other services too, for example, you can download and save comparisons of a few funds and use the details for personal analysis.

Know that these sites can be used to research details regarding ETFs as well. If you search vigilantly, you will understand the factors to consider and the factors to ignore. These online sites will act as a great pillar of support, so try to read and understand everything before you use the site. You can't handle the site if you don't know how it works, so spend some time to understand it. Also, don't think that the time spent on understanding essential things is a waste. If you want to become successful in mutual fund investing, the first step is to understand the market. The second step is to learn the market. The third step is to remain in the market even if there are a few drawbacks in the beginning. Most beginners want to make money right from the start, but it is not possible. You can never make quick money legally! So, you decide!

## Chapter 13

## Does Mutual Fund Investment Suit You?

Do you think mutual fund investment suits you? Does it match your life goals and financial goals? Of course, when we invest, we all have one goal and that is to gain returns. But it shouldn't be your only focus, and there are many other factors that you must consider before you invest your hard earned money. Before entering into the investment industry, you must ask the required questions and clear your doubts. But we often have the habit of sticking to returns without focusing on all the other essential factors as well. There are many other factors that you must consider checking to know if a mutual fund investment suit you or not.

Sometimes, beginners are misguided because they are made to believe that top funds are the ideal to consider when investing in mutual funds. They think funds that attract a higher number of investors will perform better even for a beginner. But let me ask you, do you think it's a valid assumption?

When you are selecting a mutual fund, it is good to get advice from experts, but you should do your homework as well. You might have certain financial goals and objectives, so the fund you select must meet your goals and objectives. Hence, don't blindly rely on some random funds that you "believe" as the ideal. Before you do this, you must think whether mutual fund investment suits you or not. Now, let's check out some of the points that will help you get your mind and thoughts together.

To think whether mutual fund investment suits you, it is essential to have a few financial goals. To create financial goals, you must be aware of your current financial status. Also, you must evaluate your own self before you think about investing.

Think about your investment goals. Are you interested in saving for retirement? If you are saving for retirement, you will be able to hold funds even if the market fluctuates because you are not in a hurry. If your investment goal is to buy a home, you need to pay a down payment. If you've turned to mutual fund investment for that, you'll need money in a short period of time. Even though there are funds that will help you achieve this kind of goal, you must be cautious when you invest in such funds.

Whichever funds you invest in, your investment goals should correlate with the fund. Say you are interested in playing with the daily market swings, the, you shouldn't consider funds at all. The funds are traded when the day ends so you will not get to meet your interest. When choosing a fund, you must do an in-depth analysis to decide whether it suits you or not!

Most of the time, asset allocation strategy becomes a forgotten factor. But you should not forget it. When you are selecting a fund, make sure it matches the asset allocation strategy that you have picked. Not only should you think about the asset allocation strategy, but there is also another important factor that you should think about when you decide whether or mutual fund suits you: mutual fund fees. Even though mutual funds are cost-effective when compared to other types of investments, it still has specific fees. You must be considerate about the fees because it will ruin your returns slowly, but steadily. Sometimes, fees get sneaky. If you want to ensure that you are a good fit to invest in mutual funds, you must not ignore or neglect mutual fund fees.

Certain funds don't increase diversification and don't think that more funds equal higher diversification because it does not! You must ensure that funds don't overlap, so must have the knowledge about understanding significant stock holdings of the funds. To do this, spend some time and learn about it.

You must not forget tax events because they can cause a lot of trouble as beginners, you might not feel the pressure of handling tax events, but once you get your hands on the market, you will understand. It is essential not to neglect the tax events when you are dealing with mutual fund investment. Often, you hear or read that past performances doesn't decide the future. Even in this eBook, I have mentioned it. You can't invest in a fund because it performed well last year. But by studying the way it performed, you can get some ideas and understanding about the fund. Even though you will not be able to predict the future of the fund using the details, you will still find it useful.

To make sure that you have made the right decision, you must fill your mind with the required knowledge. Pay close attention to essential details and information. For example, consider the top-rated fund companies and quality firms that deal with mutual fund investments. There are many quality firms that you can rely on, so you don't have to run out of choices. If you continue to make good choices, that means you were able to feed your mind with the right information. Even the reviewing firms will have information for you. Before you invest, you can research more about funds on your own. You can even contact a financial advisor and have a chat. When you converse and say your investment goals, current status, and knowledge about mutual fund investment, the financial advisor will help you understand whether you have made the right decision or not.

Basically, if you strongly want to do something , you never run out of choices. You find a way somehow. Just like that, if you want to make sure about your decision you have multiple resources to utilize. However, mutual fund investment will bring you benefits if you have the required knowledge about it! As we discuss the right and wrong decision, I have an essential topic to cover, which is mutual funds vs. stocks. Most beginners often debate whether they should consider stocks or mutual fund investment. Well, let's read to find out!

## Mutual Funds vs. Stocks

There are three main factors that you must consider when it comes to investing. When I say investing, I'm generalizing since it doesn't have to be mutual funds or stocks. Generally, you must consider three main factors before you invest in mutual funds or stocks. First of all, think about the risk level you can handle and the return you are looking for. Second of all, researching the investments that you have selected. You must be genuinely interested in researching the fund prospectus' or other statements. Last but not least, the third factor is about the expenses and fees you are ready to bear. There are tax implications, annual fees, commission, and more charges for different investments.

With that being said, let's learn about mutual funds and stocks and their differences. The stocks that you own is a part of a certain corporation. You can earn through dividends if you invest in stocks and it will be yearly or quarterly. There will be an annual taxable income too. Investors make money by selling stocks. You can calculate the profit by subtracting the purchase price and fees from the price it is being sold at .

As you already know, you can trade at any time of the day. Even if the market isn't in your favor, you can still move out and protect your position. Unlike stocks, mutual funds' shares are priced at the end of the day. Thus, it is a bit problematic for the investors because they can't move out of the market if the market isn't in their favor.

There are different types of funds, and the charges and fees of the funds vary as per the fund type. When selecting a fund, the investor must consider the charges and fees as well. Also, stock funds help you to consider a particularly small or large company. It is also possible to consider a geographic location or industry. The bond funds offer a fixed income, and they are less risky. But you will not get higher returns from bond funds since funds vary in different forms. The three main factors are:

**Consider The Expenses And Fees**
You will be charged a certain amount by a broker when you engage in buying and selling of stocks. The amount charged will vary as per the service providers. If you are experienced or if you have the knowledge to handle stocks on your own, you wouldn't have to bear a huge fee. If you are looking for advice to perform better, you might need to hire a broker who offers all the services. However, the full-service broker might be costly. A buy-and-hold investor doesn't have to pay a fee until he/she sells the stocks.

There will be an annual fee charged for the management of mutual funds. There are different ways of charging the fund such as when you are selling, when you are buying or sometime, a charge is not made for a certain period of time. There are no-load funds that doesn't charge any fees, but all the funds charge management fees. Plus, some funds request minimum investment too.

Most of the time, actively managed funds trade stocks often in a year. When trading stocks, if you gain capital, you must meet the tax implications. Even if the value of the fund decreases, you still have to meet tax implications. This is the main reason why investors prefer 401 (k) or IRA as their tax-advantaged accounts.

So, you must not select stocks over mutual funds or vice-versa based on random views and thoughts. Instead, you must analyze the expenses and fees that you will be charged when investing in mutual funds or stocks.

**Think About The Risk-Return**
It's apparent that mutual funds are less risky when compared to stocks. When pooling in funds or bonds together, the risk reduces when investing. For example, if one fund has a poorly performing manager and an ineffective strategy, and if the other fund has a better manager and a great strategy, the loss will be balanced accordingly. Through diversification, you will obviously face lower risks. You can get stock benefits through mutual fund investing even without involving high risks.

Hence, it is important to be aware of risk-returns when you are handling mutual funds as well as stocks.

**Be Aware Of The Availability**
The last factor is the time that you spend researching regarding the investments. It is important to research the company before you invest in stocks. Understanding the financial reports is beneficial if not crucial. When you study the financial reports, you will understand the income made by the company. Along with this, you

must be considerate about the economy as well. If you are not aware of the economy and the company's status, you will not be able to find a good company.

Although I will discuss more about creating a portfolio in the next chapter, a diversified portfolio can't be developed without enough research. You must look for companies with various strategies, different sizes, and industries. It is better to spend time researching various companies to settle for a few choices. If you already have a full-time job, you might find researching complicated. For that, you can select an investment that you can manage along with your day job.

However, for mutual funds, you don't have to spend a lot of time researching because you can get help from a manager. The manager will do the research, but that doesn't mean you have no responsibilities. You must research the promising sector to invest in, and you must know about the economy as well.

There are challenges when researching mutual funds, so you shouldn't think that it's going to be simple and easy. You can't solely rely on the manager, so as the investor you must be ready to take on the challenges in mutual funds.

After analyzing and understanding the details related to mutual funds, you will be able to decide whether it is suitable for you or not!

## Chapter 14

## Practical Advice on Building Your Portfolio

Once you have justified your decision, you can think about the next step, which is building your investment portfolio. If you think building a portfolio is simple, it is not! It takes effort, hard work, and persistent to build a portfolio. However, that's not all you need to do. You need designs tools, strategies, materials, and many other factors to build a portfolio.

The term "portfolio" is common, so it makes the beginners think that it is going to be easy. Of course, it will be easy if you gather all the necessary knowledge before investing in mutual funds. When you think about creating a portfolio, you must remember the saying, "don't put all your eggs in one basket." To create a good portfolio, you need to have a strong foundation, a good design, and a wide selection of funds that will enhance the portfolio. Remember, the selection of funds is not a simple duty because it plays a huge role in maintaining a good portfolio. Hence, you must make sure to select the right type of funds when building a portfolio. Here are some practical advice that will help you build a professional portfolio:

### Think About The Core And Satellite Portfolio Design

You will need a blueprint when building a house. The same thing goes for your portfolio since you need a portfolio design to build your own portfolio. One design is the time-tested design called Core and Satellite. This design simply means that you start with the large-cap funds to develop the larger section of your portfolio and then, you must focus on the satellite funds to develop the smaller section.

You must understand that the simplest design has the power to get the best out of your portfolio. Plus, as a beginner, instead of picking complex designs you can stick to a simple one. The Core and Satellite design is an effective, simple one that helps you in the long-run. However, the main focus of Core and Satellite is to diversify risks and to outperform for higher returns. Basically, you will be able to get above-average returns while maintaining the risks.

You must start with the core section of the design. The large-cap stock fund is a great start to diversify your portfolio. A moderate portfolio should have a percentage of 30-40%, and you can consider funds like the S&P 500 index fund. So, why do you think those core holdings is a great start? The information for large-cap index funds companies can be collected pretty easily because they are available to the general public. As the information is available to the general public, it is hard for other investors to play naïve investors. Even the experienced investors find it difficult to handle the S&P 500, so if you are facing a hard time in the beginning, don't worry!

Next, you can consider adding satellites to the portfolio. Once you are done with the core holding, the funds that represent satellites will give the final touch to the portfolio. The other funds are mid-cap stock, foreign stock, small-cap stock, sector funds, fixed income, and also money market funds. If you successfully manage these funds, you will be able to get higher returns and protect your portfolio.

Actually, the Core and Satellite design are great for the investors because they'd be able to develop a diversified portfolio. The diversifications will include different mutual funds, but the investor should be vigilant when selecting funds. Plus, investors can gain better returns through investment makeup and asset allocation.

**Don't Forget About Asset Allocation**

If you are aware of the risk tolerance level, the next important factor is asset allocation. This means the investment asset mix that is included in your portfolio. Based on the way you allocate assets; your risk tolerance can be described in different ways. They are high tolerance (aggressive), medium tolerance (moderate), and low tolerance (conservative). If you have high-risk tolerance, there will be more stocks in regard to cash and bonds in the portfolio. If you have low-risk tolerance, stocks in your portfolio will be lower when compared to cash and bonds. Hence, you must not forget about asset allocation when building your portfolio.

## Keep In Mind Your Risk Tolerance Level

If you don't know how much you can bear, you will struggle once you invest in funds out of your capacity. To create a successful portfolio, you must know the rate of risk that you are ready to tolerate. Hypothetically saying, if you lose around 10% of your $10,000 investment, will you be able to handle the loss? Both financially and emotionally? To decide whether you can or can't manage a certain risk level, you should hypothetically include an amount and think. Of course, some people can tolerate high risks, and some can't, so think about your risk tolerance level when building your portfolio.

## Dictate Your Investment Goals

This is one of the crucial parts of investing, and you must think about your investment goals before you think about anything else. Think about why you are investing, and there can be different motivations, objectives, and strategies. Sometimes, your investment goals might change with time; in that case, you should reflect on your portfolio to check whether your investment goals correlate with your portfolio.

Many young investors may be interested in generating wealth, so certain schemes match an investor's interest. In the meantime, some older investors might be interested in wealth preservations, so there are debt schemes for them. Likewise, there are different options as per the investor's interest. The simple fact that you must understand is that when building your portfolio, you must be considerate about your goals as well as your portfolio design.

## Build Your Investment Style

If you try to follow the investment style of another investor you will not be able to build your own portfolio or investment path. You might have a way of investing, and you must stick to it while focusing on other important factors like risks and returns. To build a proper portfolio, you must have the knowledge and understand the importance of it. You don't have to copy another investor's style to build a portfolio. Hence, you don't have to change your style. Instead stick to it and build a unique portfolio.

## Learn To Diversify

If you diversify without any specific reason, you will not get the actual benefit of diversifying. You must ensure the overall volatility of the portfolio, so you must trigger the key factor, which is diversification in the right way. Often, investors tend to over-diversify, so it is just as dangerous as not diversifying. One can see over-diversification among naïve investors because of the information they get. They tend to hear different things about different funds, so they blindly believe it and follow their ideas. Most of the time, beginners invest in funds that offer higher returns, but they forget about diversification and consequences. As beginners, if you want to build a successful portfolio, you must limit your selection to a five or six established mutual funds. Also, be ready to give up on certain funds if the need arises. If you set such barriers, you will be able to maintain a diverse portfolio without losing all your finances.

Nevertheless, don't stop working hard and looking for information. It is important to understand that information is an asset. If you have enough information, you can easily maintain a good mutual fund portfolio.

## Chapter 15

## FAQs on Mutual Funds

**What are mutual funds?**

Mutual funds is a collective investment. This investment lets investors invest their money together as a joint investment to handle the portfolio. The management company will administer the portfolio. The portfolio management will be handled by a custodian entity that takes care of the assets and assures the investors about the safety of the investment they have made. Unit holders means the investors who have invested in mutual funds and the investments are addressed as a number of units. The manager will mention the NAV of units.

**What do mutual funds invest in?**

They invest in securities, financial instruments, and short-term debts. But you are the one who decides what you want your mutual funds to be invested in.

## What are the possible ways to make money?
When you are dealing with mutual funds, you are offered three ways to make money. First of all, your income will be earned from dividends on bonds and stocks. A mutual fund will pay all the net income gained over a year as distribution. Secondly, it provides income through capital gains, which is by security price increment. Lastly, the increase in fund share prices is another way of making money. This happens when the price of fund holdings increases. Once it increases, you can sell them with a profit. These three ways are essential to be understood by every beginner if he or she wants to make money from mutual funds.

## What should be the fund's goal?
When you are handling certain funds, you must understand the fund's goals. You must check whether it fits your portfolio objectives. Think about the time frame that you should invest for. Consider your financial goals and check whether you get regular income from the fund. Does it match your other investments? These are the main points that you must consider when you select mutual funds. If you ensure these points, you will be able to invest confidently.

## What should be your mutual fund objectives?
Typically, an individual's objective will be to earn consistent returns with a rate of manageable risks. That said, there are mutual fund groups with specific objectives. To begin with growth funds, these funds deal with long to a medium-term time frame and capital

appreciation. Generally, growth funds are small to large-cap investments. Next is income funds; these funds deal with specific intervals while providing income. Investors who want a steady income can consider these funds. A higher percentage of investments are done in income instruments including bonds, interest debentures, dividend paying stocks, and preferred stocks. The industry or sector funds is another group of funds. These funds maximize returns by focusing on thriving sectors including health care, commodities, and real estates. The value funds are the last group out of all. These funds invest in undervalued stocks. However, you must ensure to be clear about your objectives.

## Do you think mutual funds are safe to invest?

First, what is your definition of safe? If capital protection is your definition of safe, then you can invest even though there are no returns. If that happens, you don't have to worry about safety. Unfortunately, mutual funds don't offer that sort of protection. In the investing industry, you will face risks even if you don't want to. There will be small or big risks related to investments. However, if you manage vigilantly, you will be able to invest safely. Even if you face risks, you must have the skills to manage them.

## Why should you consider mutual fund investing?

When an investor doesn't have enough time to monitor and study the market often, he orshe may consider mutual fund investing. If an individual who wants to enter the investing industry do not have the required knowledge of the financial market, he or she can consider mutual fund investing. This is an excellent opportunity to enter into the investment industry even without having knowledge about it.

## Who will manage your funds?

If you want to succeed in investing, you must know the role of a portfolio manager. The manager's role is the factor that triggers your mutual fund's success. Hence, it is essential to know the educational qualifications, experiences, and skills of the manager. Even if you don't know, it is better to ask the manager of their qualifications. You don't have to think twice to inquire about it. When questioning the manager, make sure to ask whether they manage other funds as well. Check their rate of success and how they have been managing the funds. What are their styles of investments? Don't get trapped by high turnovers because they are a warning sign. Likewise, there are a lot of factors that you must take into consideration when selecting a portfolio manager.

## What makes mutual fund investing a good choice?

There are many reasons to justify the mutual fund as the right choice. But if you want to know the main reasons, they are professional management, constant monitoring, ability to research, diversification, liquidity, transparency, tax-efficiency, regulated industry, and above all, diversification.

## What are the options offered by a mutual fund?

There are many options offered by the mutual fund, and some of them are growth option, dividend payout option, insurance plan, dividend reinvestment plan, Systematic Investment Plan (SIP), and Systematic Encashment Plan (SEP).

## What does Redemption Price mean?

When selling units (open-ended scheme) to the mutual fund, the receiver or customer obtains a certain price, so it is the redemption price.

## What does Exit Load mean?

This is imposed by a scheme to collect a certain amount from the unitholders when the scheme itself repurchases the units. The Repurchase Load is another term for Exit Load. The amount can't be charged after a certain period.

## What is switching in a mutual fund?

The chance provided to the investors to move from one scheme to another within a particular fund is called switching. By switching investor can meet their investment goals.

## Is there a fund that doesn't pay a dividend?

The fund accumulates the returns and then reinvests continuously. The main focus of this fund is to grow the NAV of each unit. Through this, investors' will be able to grow their income.

**Do you know about the investment policy?**

The management company will manage the mutual funds by adhering to the criterion of the management team and the legal frame. They will try to meet the established objectives of the funds.

For example, you must know that there are mutual funds that invest only in fixed income securities. Also, some portfolios add fixed income securities, shares, and money market instruments as well. And other funds invest in stocks and shares as they are their main interest.

Before investing, investors must make sure to select by analyzing and focusing on the investment policies of the funds. You must also ensure that the funds match your objectives. However, you must be informed about the investment policy and objectives before you invest in a mutual fund.

**What is mutual fund liquidity?**

Mutual funds allow the investors to redeem or invest whenever the investors want, and they are no limit imposed regarding this. Hence, the liquidity is great for mutual fund investment. As investors, you can liquidate whenever you want to.

**If a fund had positive returns, will it be the same this year too?**

You must accept the fact that mutual funds don't belong to fixed income products. The fund's performance will be decided upon the assets performance that are in the fund. So, if the value of the assets in the fund decreases, the value of the mutual fund investment will also decrease. You can consider the previous year's returns to study the fund's performance and quality. But you can't consider it as an indicator for future performances. You must make sure to research before you invest in a mutual fund if you want to get better returns.

## Are Mutual Fund Investments risky?

When compared to other investments, mutual fund investment is less risky. But that doesn't mean you will not face any risks when dealing with mutual funds. You might face losses when NAV declines or charges and fees are higher.

## What does a prospectus mean?

It is a document that includes information of a specific fund. The prospectus must be offered to the shareholders of the funds.

## How will you select the right mutual fund?

It is not possible to say which fund because you will have different objectives regarding mutual fund investing. Different investors have different objectives regarding mutual fund investing, hence when selecting you must focus on your objectives and aims as well. However, some investors look for aggressive growth, and some others focus on the income from bonds or stocks. Some investors consider a balanced portfolio. There are different choices available for you in the industry, so you can pick one from these choices. But you must make sure to do your research when selecting a mutual fund that suits your needs.

## How can you compare the returns (rate) between different funds?

Before you understand this question, you must make sure to get a clear understanding of the ways to compare funds. When comparing funds, it is important to compare similar types to understand relative performance. If you want to compare the returns, you must ensure that the funds are in the same category. Just like, comparing oranges to oranges. You should not compare oranges to apples.

If you compare the returns between different categories, you will not get a clear understanding, and it is pointless. Both risks and returns will be different for different categories. If you look at the financial press, you will be able to understand the performance clearly because funds are reported by type. However, even if the funds are not categorized accordingly, you must make sure to analyze accordingly.

## Should retired people consider funds?

Of course, nothing is stopping retired people from reaching out for funds. There is a certain selection of funds for retired people that will meet their investment objectives. However, it is better to focus on the conservative approach regarding the capital.

## Where can you get advice regarding investing in mutual funds?

You can get information and advice from the management team or financial advisors. Financial planning, purchase arrangements, and many other things related to investing are not easy to do without getting help from an expert. So, for that, you can seek help from financial planners, investment dealers, and fund managers as well.

## Who should consider Mutual Funds?

Almost everyone who wants to invest in mutual funds can consider it because there are no barriers. And mutual funds are suitable for all the investors. If you are a young individual who is ready to handle risks, you can consider equity schemes. The equity schemes are ideal for capital growth even though they are risky.

If you belong to the category of risk-averse individuals, you can consider income schemes. The income schemes will provide a steady income but in medium-term. Also, middle-aged individuals can utilize servings in equity and income funds. Hence, they can get capital growth and income gains. If you want to invest in mutual funds, you have different choices and opportunities. You can even meet your investment goals and objectives through these choices and opportunities.

## How will you start investing in funds?

As a beginner, this must be one of your main questions. When you are starting your journey, you must not hurry because if you do, you will not be able to manage risks. If you want to take off successfully, begin by having a defined goal, know the type of fund that will meet the financial goals, know to choose a fund at the right time, understand asset allocation, and be ready to learn whenever you are confused.

Most beginners do the opposite of what has been mentioned above. They don't want to take off smoothly and carefully, but they do want to gain excellent returns. This shouldn't be your method if you're going to begin a successful journey.

## Conclusion

Mutual fund investing might have been a new topic for you, but once you read this eBook, you'll feel like you can get started with mutual fund investing. This book contains all the required information that a beginner might need. When you are learning something for the first time, it will be tough to understand it in one sitting, but if you don't give up on your decision, you'd be able to make it happen. However, increasing your wealth is possible ONLY if you try to do it. But when you are looking for ways to increase wealth, you think of ways that don't require time and dedication. Well, if you need money you must work for it because without hard work you will not be able to earn what you want! Just like that, if you're going to enjoy more income and more wealth, you must work for it.

Most people look for income generating methods, and there is a myriad of choices. Yet, they are not convinced because they don't like to work for it. For example, mutual fund investing is considered one of the best methods to increase one's wealth. But can you invest in mutual funds without knowing what it is? Most people want to invest in mutual funds even without trying to learn it, which is not possible.

Usually, when it comes to learning about mutual funds, you will find a lot of great sources. Just because there are so many sources, it doesn't mean you will blindly select one or two sources to gather knowledge. But often, beginners make this mistake because they are eager to enter the market. Remember, rushing into things will not do you any good. Hence you must be patient. If you plan and plot, you will achieve your goals successfully. If you don't, you'll be doubtful whether you took off correctly or not. To set aside all the doubts and drawbacks, you must find the right sources to rely on. If you read this eBook, you will see how you must begin your journey as a beginner. Not only in investing but also anything that you do for the first time will be a little puzzling. Once you get the grip of what's happening around you, you'll soon become who you want to be and achieve what you want to accomplish.

As a beginner, you must make sure to learn mutual fund investing completely. It is crucial to gather knowledge on the basic information of mutual fund investing because without the basics you will stumble. Do you really want to face losses or drawbacks while trying to increase your wealth? I don't think you'd want it. Hence, I have covered all the possible information that a beginner might need. I genuinely hope Mutual Fund Investing: Comprehensive Beginners Guide to Learn the Basics and Effective Methods of Mutual Fund Investing helps you get started with mutual fund investing!

Cheers to a successful journey!

# Reference

Chen, J. (2018). Fund Manager. Retrieved from
    https://www.investopedia.com/terms/f/fundmanager.asp

Mcwhinney, J. (2018). A Brief History of the Mutual Fund. Retrieved
    https://www.investopedia.com/articles/mutualfund/05/mfhistory.asp

Load vs. No-load Mutual Fund: What's the Difference? (2019). Retrieved from
    https://www.investopedia.com/ask/answers/125.asp

Made in the USA
Coppell, TX
12 September 2022